EXPLORING THEMES

AN INTERACTIVE APPROACH TO LITERATURE

Patricia A. Richard-Amato

Longman

Exploring Themes: An Interactive Approach to Literature

Credits appear on page 165.

Acquisitions director: Joanne Dresner
Development editor: Louisa Hellegers
Production editor: Lisa Hutchins
Text design: The Wheetley Company, Inc.
Cover design: Joseph DePinho
Cover photo: National Museum of American Art, Washington, D.C./Art Resource, New York: Asher Brown Durand, *Dover Plains, Dutchess County, New York.*
Text art: Jay Benson, Carol Burger, Susan McDonald, Greg Newson, Den Schofield
Photo research: Polli Heyden
Production supervisor: Richard Bretan

ISBN 0-8013-1315-5

4 5 6 7 8 9 10-CRS-97 96 95

For my Sister
Jennifer Abbott Johnson

CONTENTS

TO THE TEACHER

What Approach Is Used in this Book?

In this book, an interactive approach is used to teach literature. Such an approach requires an interplay between reader and text and between reader and others in the classroom and its surroundings. The skills (in this case, those related to reading) are taught through a focus on the reader. The reader's prior knowledge, culture, valuing systems, relationships, dreams, and goals are explored in relation to ten universal themes.

This book treats skills not as isolated elements to master but as strategies used to comprehend and extend the meaning of the readings.

What Skills Are Included?

The chart below lists the reading skills that receive special emphasis in this book and the units in which each is found. The chart is not meant to imply either that the list is all-inclusive or that these particular skills are reinforced only in the indicated units. On the contrary, a wide variety of skills including reading, writing, speaking, thinking, and, listening are integrated throughout the book.

Skills Development Summary	UNITS									
	1	2	3	4	5	6	7	8	9	10
Thinking about Your Prereading Reactions	✓	✓	✓	✓	✓	✓	✓	✓	✓	✓
Understanding Intended Meaning	✓	✓	✓	✓	✓	✓	✓	✓	✓	✓
Making Inferences	✓		✓			✓			✓	✓
Reading Critically						✓				✓
Determining the Main Idea		✓			✓		✓			
Developing Your Word Bank	✓	✓	✓	✓	✓	✓	✓	✓	✓	✓
Appreciating Descriptive Language		✓		✓	✓		✓		✓	✓
Taking Liberty with Language					✓					
Finding Information to Support Conclusions		✓								
Drawing Comparisons	✓				✓		✓	✓	✓	✓
Using a Continuum to Clarify Ideas							✓			
Comparing Cultural Expectations	✓	✓	✓			✓	✓		✓	✓
Relating to Self or Personal Experience			✓	✓	✓	✓	✓	✓	✓	✓

Skills Development Summary	UNITS									
	1	2	3	4	5	6	7	8	9	10
Taking a Closer Look at Attitudes	✓									
Identifying Point of View			✓					✓		✓
Exploring the Conflict				✓				✓		
Identifying the Setting			✓							
Discovering the Character				✓	✓	✓				
Predicting Events						✓				
Tracking the Plot of a Story			✓					✓		
Detecting Foreshadowing						✓		✓		

For Whom Is the Book Intended?

The book is intended for older adolescent and adult students who are operating at high-intermediate and advanced levels in English as a second or foreign language. Many are preparing for study in various fields at English-speaking colleges or universities.

What Kinds of Readings Are Presented?

The readings include stories, short essays, biographical and autobiographical sketches, an excerpt from a short novel, poems, songs, and cartoons. All are organized around ten universal themes: To A Distant Shore, The Journey Back, Letting Go, All That Glitters, The Power of Illusion, Between Two Cultures, The Search for Love, Survival, Simple Pleasures, and Images of Growing Old. Authors whose works are represented include Thomas Whitecloud, Howard Maier, John Steinbeck, Kahlil Gibran, Jack London, Anne Morrow Lindbergh, Elizabeth Yates, and many more.

What Sorts of Activities Are Included?

In order that it have the best possible chance for becoming internalized, content must be explored in sufficient depth that the reader can experience its presence, reflect upon its substance, and expand upon its meaning. The activities in each unit are designed to aid in this process. In addition, they will help students become skilled readers of literature by increasing basic comprehension.

All the units begin with prereading questions that act as starters to get students into the selections and to help them relate the selections to prior knowledge and experience. Through this means, key concepts are introduced. In addition to using the prereading questions, the teacher may wish to introduce students to the unit theme by listing a few key words on the chalkboard or on an overhead transparency. The students can then say anything that comes to mind relating to these words while the teacher records the associations for all to see and asks questions to clarify and/or extend meaning. In addition, teachers might call students' attention to titles, pictures, headings, and any other features of the text that offer clues to the content.

The activities following each selection encourage the progressive development of higher-order thinking skills. Each unit begins at the knowledge level and moves slowly toward more demanding, less context-embedded ways of thinking and operating. Each unit builds upon the preceding ones as the students stretch to increasingly higher levels. Eventually, the students gain confidence in their abilities to analyze, synthesize, and evaluate what they read.

Each unit ends with ideas for discussion and writing which take the students beyond the text and the classroom, often to other settings and other resources.

Most of the activities and ideas can be easily modified in whatever ways seem appropriate for particular classes and situations. Those meant for discussion can often be used as written work, and vice versa. Those intended for pair work can be adapted for use with larger groups. Students who do not feel comfortable with a particular activity, for whatever reason, should not be required to participate. Activities that are not culturally appropriate or suited to the needs of specific groups may be eliminated altogether.

How Are the Units Organized?

The units have been arranged so as to maximize the students' feelings of success. Important considerations included (1) natural reinforcement of concepts, structures, and skills and (2) difficulty levels, both semantic and syntactic. However, because judgments in these matters are complicated and highly subjective, the prudent teacher will not feel bound to the present arrangement but will change it as he or she sees fit. In addition, not all units need to be included. The decision whether or not to use a specific unit should be based on students' needs and interests.

How Should New Vocabulary Be Approached?

As mentioned previously, key concepts are generally presented in the prereading activities. However, the students will need effective strategies to enable them to deal with unfamiliar vocabulary within the readings themselves.*

In most situations the following strategies appear to work best. Encourage the students to:

1. *Read.* Have the students read each selection through first, without consciously stopping to figure out every unfamiliar word or phrase. Point out that good readers look for overall meaning and are not concerned about every new element. Remind students that new words and phrases often become clear from understanding the context in which they are found.

One word of caution here. If there appear to be too many unfamiliar elements for particular students, these students may need to be given lower-level materials at first. See other titles in the Longman series.

2. *Reread for Greater Understanding.* As part of the activities following the readings, students will generally be asked to reread the selections for greater understanding. This time, they should make a more conscious effort to guess the meanings of words and phrases that remain puzzling. Have them write in pencil some of their guesses above or beside each word or phrase. They should return to the context for clues. At this point, students may need to check the definitions and clues for particular words or phrases found at the bottom of the pages or in the Glossary at the back of the book. For students' convenience, the Glossary consists of an alphabetical listing of the definitions found at the bottom of the pages. In cases where pronunciation is indicated, the transcriptions are consistent with those of most English dictionaries used today. Note that numbers found beside words in the text refer to the Notes at the end of each unit.

3. *Discuss and/or Look Up Unfamiliar Elements.* If particular words or phrases are still unclear, have students discuss them with each other or with you. They could also look up such words in a dictionary. Note that the dictionary may give several different meanings for one word. Refer students back to the context to make sure they have chosen the appropriate meaning.

Toward the end of each unit is an activity entitled Developing Your Word Bank. Here students are asked to pay close attention to those words and phrases in the reading selections with which they were at first unfamiliar. Then they are to list a few of these items in the Word Bank at the end of the book. They are encouraged to work with a partner or have their teacher help them in this task. The students should list only those elements that they feel will be useful in conversation, in writing, or in communication about an academic area in which they have a special interest. Thus, the students' vocabulary work is tailored to their individual needs and interests.

What about Reading Aloud?

Forcing students to read aloud often interferes with the normal reading process and creates anxiety.

Reading aloud is a very specialized skill that should be attempted only by volunteers and only after a selection has been read silently and its meaning comprehended. Easily understood stories, plays, poetry, and other pieces may, however, be read aloud by the teacher, other experienced readers, or volunteers. Remember that in most situations reading is a very personal activity that requires uninterrupted time in a quiet, comfortable, nonthreatening atmosphere either at home or in the classroom.

Conclusion

This book aims to provide pleasurable experiences in reading literature through an interactive approach to skills development. Individual teachers can facilitate the learning process by providing a supportive environment in which students explore their inner resources in relation to the content and to one another, thereby reaching higher and higher levels of understanding.

TO THE STUDENT

In this book you will read literature about people, their experiences, and their differing value systems and ways of thinking. You will be introduced to a variety of real and imagined people: a young college student returning home, only to have unexpected feelings surface within him; a woman whose island vacation alone causes her to examine what her life has become; an unprepared traveler in the frozen north who faces almost certain death. Adjusting to new cultural surroundings, finding and keeping love, growing old, and survival are only a few of the important themes explored. Through stories, poetry, songs, short essays, cartoons, and written sketches about real people, you will get to know some of their deepest thoughts, including their joys, fears, inner conflicts, and triumphs.

The activities before and after each selection will help you to discover meaning at several different levels and to develop many of the skills needed to understand what you read. Exploring conflict, discovering the character, appreciating descriptive language, and reading critically are only a few of the skill areas in which you will work. Some activities ask for the bare facts about a reading. But most of the activities, in one way or another, ask you to think about the readings in relation to your own life and the lives of others around you. During many activities you will work alone. During others you will work with a partner or a small group. Your teacher will serve as your guide.

You will be asked to develop your own Word Bank in which you can store new or unfamiliar words and phrases. In your Word Bank you should only list those elements from the readings that you feel will be useful in conversation, in writing, or in communication about an academic area in which you have a special interest. Thus, your vocabulary work will focus on your own needs and interests.

While you are on this journey into literature, you will improve your reading and thinking skills in English—not through drill and exercises, but through understanding and reflection. This book has been designed for your pleasure as well as for your learning.

ACKNOWLEDGMENTS

I wish to express my appreciation to the following people whose comments and suggestions were invaluable during the initial stages of this book's development: Sue Gould, Martha Bean, Carol Numrich, and Linda Robinson. Also to Sharyn Moore at the ELS Language Center in Santa Monica, who field-tested a representative portion of the materials and shared her ideas with me. I am also very grateful to Joanne Dresner, Debbie Goldblatt, Louisa Hellegers, and Lisa Hutchins, editors at Addison-Wesley/Longman, who understood my purpose and were very supportive and helpful all along the way. Many thanks also to Polli Heyden, who assisted in collecting photographs and in tracking down wayward permissions. Finally, a special thank you to my husband, Jay, and to my parents, who gave me much encouragement.

UNIT

1

TO A DISTANT SHORE

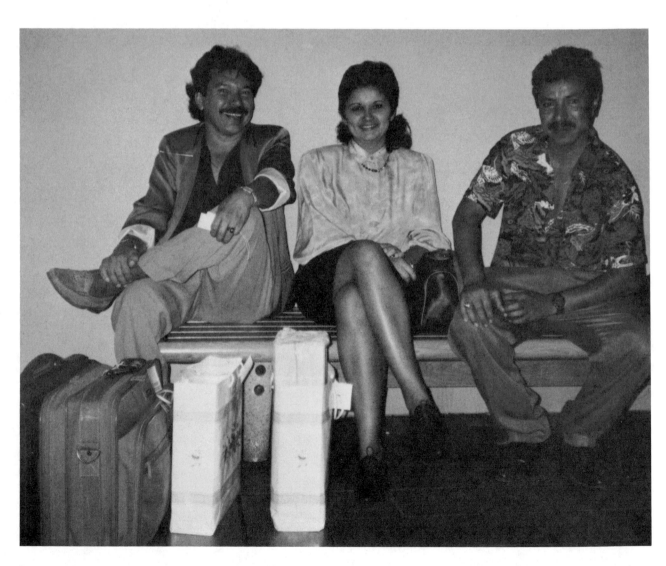

Think about your own situation. Have you recently arrived on a "distant shore"? Are you planning to make such a move? Even if you cannot answer yes to either question, try to imagine what it might be like to leave your home and live far away. What joys are experienced by persons going from one culture to another? What problems do they face? Discuss with your class.

In this unit four newcomers to the United States share their stories—why they came to the United States in the first place and what feelings they now have about the move. You might be in for some surprises.

from **Home of the Brave:**
Contemporary American Immigrants
Mary Motley Kalergis (editor)

Varuni Nelson

I was born in Sri Lanka, but as a young child my parents moved to England to complete their medical training. When we moved back to Sri Lanka, I had forgotten my Sinhala[1] and could only speak English. I kept up my studies in English even though the government was encouraging classes to be taught in the native language. My family moved to Zambia, in Africa, and there was a lot of resentment against Indians and English-speaking people because the country had recently gained independence. It was not a very pleasant experience. The United States began to look like the best place for us to live because we spoke English and they were looking for doctors. It's almost like I was an immigrant all my life, so I was grateful and happy to go to the United States. I knew the country was more welcoming toward immigrants. After the move, it took me several years to realize that I was living in a country that I wasn't passing through, that I'd stay and become a citizen. I consider myself an American, but I'll wear a sari[2] when I get married next year. I could not see myself in the typical American white wedding veil, even though I wear dresses to work. I know I've really become an American because I'm not nearly as critical of this country's arrogance as I was when I first came here. I used to think it was ludicrous that the World Series[3] was called the World Series when it was only played with American teams. Now I'm such a baseball fan, I don't stop to think about such things.

One way my life will be different here in America for me than it was for my mother is that it was a lot easier for educated middle-class women to work

---

resentment: *A feeling of anger toward something or someone thought to be the cause of one's emotional or physical pain. ". . . against Indians and English-speaking people because the country had recently gained independence" is a clue.*

immigrant: *A person who comes into a country to live permanently (im- means in; -migra- refers to moving). This label is different from*

the refugee *label, which means that the person does not have a country to go to for a period of time.*

arrogance: *The state of being filled with self-importance. The following sentence is a clue.*

ludicrous: *Absurd or laughable. The rest of the sentence is a clue.*

outside the home in Sri Lanka because domestic help was so easily available. Even mothers with young children didn't feel guilty about leaving their babies with someone else while they went out because everyone else did it too. American women seem a lot more confused about being a mother and having a career. It didn't seem unusual at all for me growing up that my mother was a doctor because my parents had met each other in medical school and most of their friends were doctors. Almost all of my childhood friends had live-in domestic help. That seems to be something only the very wealthy have here, and it makes it harder for middle-class women to work outside the home.

I realized by my teens that I was too squeamish to be a doctor, but I'd always loved words and language. I knew it wasn't practical to be a writer, so law school seemed like a good step after college. I'm a lawyer now and I like the intellectual challenge and the security of the work. America is a wonderful country for capable, ambitious people, but a lot of people also fall through the cracks. The upside of this country is it offers different kinds of people different opportunities, but the downside is its complacency about being the greatest country on Earth. There's still plenty of room for improvement.

Understanding Intended Meaning

Discuss the following questions with your class.

1. What happened to Varuni Nelson's family in Zambia that was very unpleasant?

2. Why did Varuni want to come to the United States? Is she critical of the United States? Explain.

3. Why did Varuni become a lawyer rather than a doctor? Was this a good decision, according to her? Explain.

---

domestic: Referring to the home or household (domes- means house).
squeamish: Easily sickened.
fall through the cracks: Are ignored.

upside/downside: Positive side/negative side.
complacency: Self-satisfaction. ". . . about being the greatest country on Earth" is a clue.

Thuhuong Nguyen

I was just a little child during the Vietnam War. I remember the sounds of the bombs—running, running, dead bodies and blood and I don't know where I'm running to. This is one of the earliest memories of my childhood. When I was fourteen years old, my mother told me to go with these people and get on a boat. I didn't know who they were or where I was going, but I was brought up to do what I was told. When I got on the boat, it was horrible—dark and cramped, with no food and water. For six days it was too crowded to even lie down. We finally made it to a refugee camp in Galang.[4] They gave us just enough food to keep us alive. I spent ten months there and it kept getting more and more crowded with refugees arriving every day. All I could do was hold on to the idea of America as a place that would save my life.

I have so much family still in Vietnam who are in a desperate situation. I send them as much money as I can. It makes it hard to save for college, but I am so much better off than they are that I can't say no to their needs. If I could get a college degree, I could make more money to send them, but it's impossible to save up enough for the tuition. I work six days a week, over twelve hours a day. Sometimes I feel so bad. I'm afraid my life will pass by and I'll never be able to get an education or have a family. My brother in Oregon wants to give me some money for college, but he needs that money for his own family and I really do want to take care of myself.

I like my independence but sometimes it feels a bit lonely. People here aren't so friendly toward me. Sometimes I feel invisible, like they see right through me. Now that I can speak English, I still don't feel totally accepted here. I used to think that it was just a language problem, but I'm afraid the problem is bigger than that. I think some people resent me because I'm Vietnamese.

Understanding Intended Meaning

Discuss the following questions with your class.

1. Describe Thuhuong Nguyen's experiences before coming to the United States. Do you think her experiences are typical of other refugees? Explain.

2. What seem to be Thuhuong's two most important goals? Do you think that she will eventually be able to achieve them? Why or why not?

3. Does Thuhuong feel accepted by the people in her new homeland? Explain.

---

cramped: *Crowded.*
refugee camp: *A place where people who do not have a country to go to can live temporarily and receive basic necessities for living.*

tuition: *The money that a person pays to go to a public college or university or to a private school.*

Christopher Auguste

As a boy in Trinidad, I had a pretty bourgeois upbringing. We owned our home and had one of the first TVs in our town. Then my father lost his job, and it soon became apparent that if we were going to regain our standard of living, we would have to leave the island. My parents' marriage collapsed, and my father went to the United States, leaving my mother back in Trinidad with seven children. My oldest three brothers came to America to get jobs and eventually we all came. We got an apartment in Harlem, where I found myself segregated by color for the first time. Race was obviously an issue here. I was treated as a black. People on the subway would keep their eye on me. I got a scholarship to Andover[5] from my junior high school in Harlem. It wasn't a hard transition for me. I'd grown up in the British school system in Trinidad. I was used to open green spaces and soccer—things that were totally unfamiliar to most kids in Harlem. Also, being an immigrant, I really valued my education because I knew it was my way out of poverty. It was no big deal for me to do a couple hours of homework every day. I was treated as exotic and interesting at prep school because of my accent and my ability to play soccer. It was a bit strange hearing about my friends' ski trips to the Alps,[6] and when I'd go home for vacation my mother's on welfare and the apartment had no heat. It's amazing, though, my family really never sank to the depths of despair; we never considered our poverty anything but a temporary situation. My mother was always so grateful for my good fortune; I never felt guilty to have the opportunity for a good education. After graduation, I went to Harvard[7] and Harvard Law School. By the time I was in college, my mother had a job and had saved enough to own her own home. Education and home ownership were two of our biggest dreams. It never occurred to us that we couldn't achieve our dreams if we worked hard. My mother didn't lose one of us to the streets. All of us were able to get jobs and establish ourselves. I probably worked much harder in school because I was an immigrant. I was much hungrier for success. I wanted to prove I was good enough to compete with anyone. I always wanted to maintain my West Indian identity. At Harvard, I started a Caribbean Club. My culture is distinctly different from black Americans, and I felt it was important to distinguish the difference.

Coming from a small island, we had to learn about the rest of the world. Geography is a very important subject in school. Here in America, they are too chauvinistic to learn about other countries. The world looks toward America much more than America looks out toward the world.

I have no delusions about how the system works here. It's still dominated by white males. In my law firm there are about fourteen black attorneys out of two hundred sixty lawyers. I'm glad to be there, but I also know that there's only one black partner out of seventy. The question is

---

bourgeois: *(pronounced "bōor-zhwä'") The middle class. "We owned our home" is a clue.*
apparent: *Obvious or visible (appar- refers to appearing).*
standard of living: *The economic level at which one lives.*
collapsed: *Fell into ruin or broke down.*
segregated: *Separated (se- means apart; -greg- refers to a herd or flock). ". . . by color" is a clue.*
exotic: *Unfamiliar and exciting (ex- means outside).*

prep school: *A school that prepares students for college.*
despair: *To lose all hope. ". . . sank to the depths of " is a clue.*
distinctly: *In a well-defined way (distin- refers to separating).*
chauvinistic: *Believing that one's own group is superior to others. ". . . to learn about other countries" is a clue.*
delusions: *False beliefs (de- means away from). ". . . about how the system works here" is a clue.*
dominated: *Controlled (domina- refers to a lord or master).*

how many people can break through the color barrier. Opportunity is what people need—not guarantees. This country probably provides more opportunity to immigrants than it does black Americans who were born here in a poverty that's lasted for generations. Second- and third-generation welfare breeds a despair that America's immigrants are free of. We come here because we really believe we can make it, and that hopefulness gives us a better chance at it.

Understanding Intended Meaning

Discuss the following questions with your class.

1. Briefly describe Christopher Auguste's life in Trinidad.

2. What unexpected treatment was in store for Christopher when he moved to Harlem. Why? What seemed to especially bother him about this treatment?

3. How did Christopher's family deal with its poverty? What did Christopher think was his way out of poverty?

4. To what factors does Christopher credit his success?

color barrier: Obstacles because of one's race. ". . . people can break through" is a clue.
breeds: Gives birth to.

Naoto Nakagawa

My grandfather was a very well-known painter and scholar in Japan. The family story goes that when his house was bombed during the war, it burned for three days and nights because he had so many books and papers. My allegiance was always to art, even as a young boy. I held no grudge against the United States.[8] I wanted to paint. After the war, by the end of the 1950s, New York clearly emerged as the center of the art world. I was shocked by the people's ignorance about Japan when I arrived here over twenty years ago. We knew so much about America, but they didn't know much about us. Of course, now, all the major cities have been "sushi-ized," but it was quite different back then.

The first few years here were very difficult, but I was lucky that people responded to my paintings right away, even though I was very raw and angry at that time. It was very frustrating for me when I couldn't paint full-time. I had to work at any job I could get, then came home too exhausted to paint. I got my first exhibition five years after I came to this country. I got good reviews and things began to change. I was invited to museum group shows and galleries, but my financial hardship continued for many years after my first critical recognition. The art world was different back then. I fear for American art today because there is so much

hype and greed. Fame and financial success can overwhelm creativity. America seems to be a failure when it comes to nurturing a great artist. Jackson Pollock[9] was completely unable to paint during the last years of his life. He was overwhelmed by his reputation. America's visual arts don't seem to have a tradition of being in touch with the deepest part of oneself and knowing how to express that on the canvas. Like American cars when they are new and beautiful, everyone wants a ride, but the other side of the coin is the junkyard. It just gets used up and put aside. This can happen to art that is mainly concerned with surface technique and trends.

I feel very fortunate to have the resources of two great cultures. To this day I still draw great inspiration from my childhood in Japan. These primary memories are the foundation of my art. The beauty of nature had a profound effect on my relationship with the world. I didn't have the toys or TV that American children had, but I learned how to catch fish with my bare hands and dragonflies with a rock and string. I'll never forget the red sunsets with thousands of bats flying in the sky. I can really see how Shintoism[10] developed in Japan. Everything in nature is God. Every rock and tree and leaf in the woods has spirit. I learned this as a boy, when mud was my toy. I don't paint in the Western tradition of

---

scholar: *A highly educated person* (schol- *means school*).
allegiance: *Loyalty.*
grudge: *A deep-seated resentment.* ". . . *against the United States" is a clue.*
emerged: *Came up out of* (e- *means out;* -merge- *means to dip*).
sushi-ized: *An invented word similar to the word "modernized"* (sushi *is raw fish;* -ized *here means to be accepted as a practice*).
raw: *Here it means inexperienced.*
exhibition: *A show or display for the public* (ex- *means out;* -hibi- *refers to holding*).
reviews: *Here it means reports in newspapers or magazines that tell the*

reporters' views of the strengths and weaknesses of a piece of work.
galleries: *Buildings in which artwork is displayed for public view.*
critical: *Here it means serious and important.*
hype: *Overrating something in order to sell it.*
overwhelm: *Overcome or overpower.*
nurturing: *Helping to develop* (nurtu- *refers to feeding*).
the other side of the coin: *The opposite of something.*
inspiration: *Something that encourages another to act.*
primary: *Here it means most important* (prim- *means first*).
profound: *Deep.*

still life. I see the objects on my canvas as glorious, living things. I'm conscious of the spirit of the natural objects in my paintings, not just the form and surface. My highest goal is getting in touch with the glory of creation.

The reason I wanted to live and paint in America is that there are no rules of tradition. Here we are free to create our own traditions. I can draw from the resources of Eastern art, but I can also break away and take my painting in any direction I want. Freedom is America's greatest contribution. Freedom of thought and expression is the most valuable thing that this country has to offer. America has a big heart. It accepts, even encourages, people's differences.

Understanding Intended Meaning

Discuss the following questions with your class.

1. What does Naoto Nakagawa think of American art? Does he like it? How do you know? Near the end of the second paragraph, to what does Naoto compare American art?

2. What is Naoto's highest goal? Explain.

3. Why does Naoto want to be an artist in America? What does he feel is America's greatest contribution to people who want to create?

Thinking about Your Prereading Reactions

Return to the questions on page 3. Think again about your answers to the questions. Were the joys and problems that you connected with moving to a distant shore similar to those experienced by the newcomers whose stories you read in this unit?

Drawing Comparisons

It is interesting to compare the situations, goals, and other characteristics of the four newcomers. A Venn diagram[11] has been used on the next page to begin a comparison between Varuni Nelson and Thuhuong Nguyen. Notice that the things Varuni and Thuhuong have in common have been placed in the overlapping area of the circles. Work with a partner to complete the diagram.

---

still life: An art style in which all subjects are lifeless.
glorious: Deserving glory or highest praise.

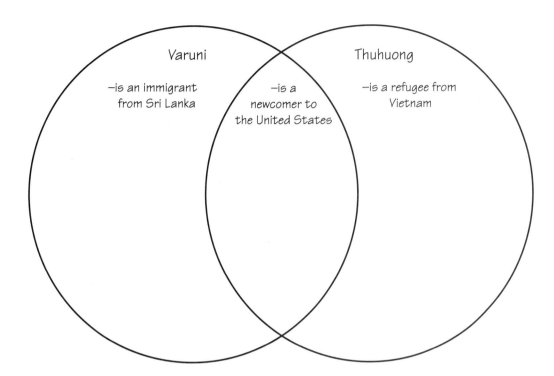

Now work with a partner and use the Venn diagram below to draw a comparison between two newcomers of your choice.

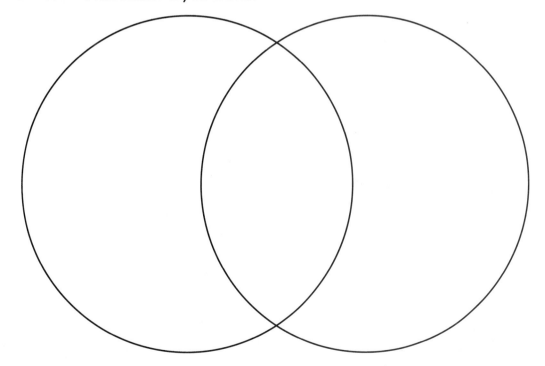

Form a group with at least two other people and share your diagrams. You may want to make changes in them based on what you learn from the others in your group.

Taking a Closer Look at Attitudes

It is clear from the reading selections that the newcomers' attitudes toward the United States are mixed. Some attitudes tend to be more positive; others, more negative. Read the quotes in the first column below. Then decide whether each is more positive or negative and check the appropriate column. Last, briefly state your own reaction to each quote—for example, do you agree or disagree with the statement being made?

Quote	Positive	Negative	Your Reaction
Varuni Nelson said:			
1. "I knew the country [the United States] was more welcoming toward immigrants [than other countries]" (page 4).			
2. "America is a wonderful country for capable, ambitious people" (page 5).			
3. ". . . but a lot of people also fall through the cracks" (page 5).			
Thuhuong Nguyen said:			
4. "People here aren't so friendly toward me" (page 6).			
5. "I think some people resent me because I'm Vietnamese" (page 6).			
Christopher Auguste said:			
6. "Race was obviously an issue here [in the United States]" (page 8).			
7. "Here in America, they [the people] are too chauvinistic to learn about other countries" (page 8).			
8. "I have no delusions about how the system works here [in the United States]. It's still dominated by white males" (page 8).			

Quote	Positive	Negative	Your Reaction
Naoto Nakagawa said:			
9. "I was shocked by the people's ignorance about Japan when I arrived here [in the United States] over twenty years ago" (page 11).			
10. "I fear for American art today because there is so much hype and greed" (page 11).			
11. "The reason I wanted to live and paint in America is that there are no rules of tradition" (page 12).			
12. "Freedom is America's greatest contribution. Freedom of thought and expression is the most valuable thing that this country has to offer" (page 12).			
13. "America has a big heart. It accepts, even encourages, people's differences" (page 12).			

Do any of the newcomers agree on any points of comparison? Do you see any direct contradictions? Explain. Choose two or three of the quotes above to discuss with a small group. Talk about your reactions and relate the quotes to your own experiences whenever possible.

Making Inferences

Discuss the following questions with your class.

1. According to Varuni Nelson, what advantage does Sri Lanka have for working middle class mothers? What do you think this means for those people who are below the middle class in Sri Lanka?

2. Varuni felt that in Zambia there was "resentment against Indians and English-speaking people because the country had recently gained independence." Why might the fact that they had recently gained independence cause their resentment? Do you know of other places where a similar situation exists or has existed? Explain.

3. Varuni said that although she "loved words and language, . . . it wasn't practical to be a writer." What does she mean? Do you think writing is a practical profession? Explain.

4. According to Christopher Auguste, "Second- and third-generation welfare breeds a despair that America's immigrants are free of." What does he mean? Do you agree? Explain.

Comparing Cultural Expectations

Discuss two or more of the following questions with a small group.

1. Varuni Nelson reports that she forgot her native Sinhala while living in England. How important do you think it is to remember one's native language? Explain.

2. For what reasons do you think Christopher Auguste wants to maintain his West Indian identity? To what extent do you think the other newcomers want to maintain their original identities? Do you think it is important for them to do so? Why or why not?

3. Christopher claims that he was sometimes treated as "exotic" in his new country. Have you ever been treated this way? If so, how did such treatment make you feel? Why do you think you were treated this way?

4. Naoto Nakagawa tells of an American artist who was unable to produce because he was "overwhelmed by his reputation." What does Naoto mean? Do you think this happens often? Does this happen in the culture you know best? Explain.

5. How does Naoto compare childhood in Japan with childhood in America? Do you agree with his conclusions? How would you compare your own childhood with childhood in America? How would you compare it with childhood in Japan when Naoto lived there?

6. Naoto feels that America "accepts, even encourages, people's differences." How important is it to accept and encourage differences? Are differences accepted and encouraged in the culture you know best? Explain.

Developing Your Word Bank

One way to increase your vocabulary is to pay close attention to those words and phrases in a reading selection with which you were at first unfamiliar. Many of the more common words and phrases used in this unit reappear in other selections throughout the book. Make a Word Bank (see page 152) listing a few of the words or phrases that are new to you. Choose only those items that you feel will be useful. You may want to work with a partner or have your teacher help you with this task. Consider words you might want to use in conversation, in writing, or in communication about an academic area in which you have a special interest.

Ideas for Discussion and/or Writing

Choose one or more of the following activities.

1. Write your own life story. You might want to use one of the stories from this unit as a guide. In your story, tell about your own life, current situation, experiences with distant shores, and so on. Bring to class a photo of yourself and perhaps one of family members. With your classmates put together a class scrapbook to share with others.

2. Are you now on a distant shore? If so, write several questions to ask others who are in a similar situation. Following are a few sample questions.

   ◆ Where are you from?
   ◆ Why did you come to this country? How long have you been here?
   ◆ What were the joys you experienced upon first arriving?
   ◆ Did you face any problems? If so, what were they?
   ◆ To what extent have you been able to overcome your problems?

3. If you are now on a distant shore, begin a journal in which you make entries two or three times a week. Include reflections on your own experiences with your new language and culture and anything else you want to write. If you are not now on a distant shore, you may want to keep a journal of your reactions to the reading selections in this book instead. Include also your reflections on your own progress with the English language. Share your journal with your teacher from time to time if you wish.

4. Choose one or more of the feelings expressed by the newcomers in the quotes on pages 14–15. Write one or more paragraphs using the feeling(s) as a topic. When you are finished, share your writing with a partner. Ask your partner to write a brief response, including areas of agreement or disagreement. You may want to react in writing to your partner's response, thus continuing the discussion in writing.

Notes

1. Sinhala is the Indic language of Sri Lanka.
2. A sari is a long piece of cloth wrapped around the head and body.
3. The World Series is the group of championship professional baseball games played each fall in the United States.
4. Refers to Galang Besar, which is an island below Singapore.
5. Andover is a school in Andover, Massachusetts, that prepares students for college.
6. The Alps are a group of mountains in south central Europe.
7. Harvard is the oldest institution of higher learning in the United States. It is located in Cambridge, Massachusetts.
8. Refers to the bombing of Japan by the United States near the end of World War II.
9. Jackson Pollock (1912–1956) was a modern American artist whose technique included dripping paint on canvas. He worked with sticks rather than brushes.
10. Shintoism is the native religion of Japan.
11. The Venn diagram was developed in 1880 by a British logician named John Venn. It is used to clarify comparisons.

2

THE JOURNEY BACK

First Christmas

Stan Rogers

This day, a year ago, he was rolling in the snow

With a younger brother, in his father's yard.

Christmas break—a time for touching home

The heart of all he'd known, and leaving was so hard—

Three thousand miles away, now he's working Christmas Day

Making double time for the "minding of the store" . . .

Well, he always said he'd make it on his own

He's spending Christmas Eve alone.

First Christmas away from home.

In the United States and elsewhere, Christmas Eve (the night before Christmas) is often a time when Christians (and others) get together with family and close friends. They may exchange gifts, eat special foods, and/or attend religious gatherings. Because much importance is placed on being with family members at Christmas, being away from home is especially difficult at this time of the year. Are similar holidays celebrated in the culture you know best?

Like the young man in the song "First Christmas," people sometimes find themselves far away from home and from those they love. Many dream of returning one day. Think about your own situation. Are you now far away from home? If not, imagine that you are. What do you think might happen if you returned home after a long time away? What would be the joys? Might there also be some fear? If so, why? Discuss with your class.

making double time: Getting paid double the regular pay.
minding of the store: Managing of the store.

make it on his own: Live independently.

Often dreams of returning home come true. In this unit Thomas Whitecloud, an American Indian, tells a story about his return to the reservation where he grew up. His visit, however, turns out somewhat differently than he expects.

from Blue Winds Dancing

Thomas Whitecloud

Morning. I spend the day cleaning up and buying some presents for my family with what is left of my money. Nothing much, but a gift is a gift, if a man buys it with his last quarter. I wait until evening, then start up the railroad track toward home.

Christmas Eve comes in on a north wind. Snow clouds hang over the pines, and the night comes early. Walking along the railroad bed, I feel the calm peace of snowbound forests on either side of me. I take my time; I am back in a world where time does not mean so much now.

I am alone—alone but not nearly so lonely as I was back on the campus at school. Those are never lonely who love the snow and the pines, never lonely when the pines are wearing white shawls and snow crunches coldly underfoot.

In the woods I know there are the tracks of deer and rabbits. I know that if I leave the rails and go into the woods, I shall find them. I walk along feeling glad because my legs are light and my feet seem to know that they are home. A deer comes out of the woods just ahead of me and stands silhouetted on the rails. The North, I feel, has welcomed me home. I watch him and am glad that I do not wish for a gun. He goes into the woods quietly, leaving only the design of his tracks in the snow.

I walk on. Now and then I pass a field, white under the night sky, with houses at the far end. Smoke comes from the chimneys of the houses, and I try to tell what sort of wood each is burning by the smoke. There is one from which comes black coal smoke that rises lazily and drifts out over the tops of the trees. I like to watch houses and try to imagine what might be happening in them.

---

pines: *A type of evergreen tree.*
shawls: *Loose coverings women sometimes wear over their heads and shoulders to provide warmth.*
crunches: *Makes a crushing sound. "... coldly underfoot" is a clue.*

silhouetted: *(pronounced "sĭl-o͞o-ĕt-ĭd") Appearing to be outlined and filled in with black.*
drifts: *Flows gently. "... out over the tops of the trees" is a clue.*

Just as a light snow begins to fall, I cross the reservation boundary. Somehow it seems as though I have stepped into another world. Deep woods in a white-and-black winter night. A faint trail leading to the village.

The railroad on which I stand comes from a city sprawled by a lake—a city with a million people who walk around without seeing one another; a city sucking the life from all the country around; a city with stores and police and intellectuals and criminals and movies and apartment houses; a city with its politics and libraries and zoos.

Laughing, I go into the woods. As I cross a frozen lake, I begin to hear the drums. Soft in the night the drums beat. It is like the pulse beat of the world. The white line of the lake ends at a black forest, and above the trees the blue winds are dancing.

I come to the outlying houses of the village. Simple box houses, etched black in the night. From one or two windows soft lamplight falls on the snow. Christmas is here, too, but it does not mean much—not much in the way of parties and presents. Joe Sky will get drunk. Alex Bodidash will buy his children red mittens and a new sled. Alex is a college man and tries to keep his home up to white standards. White standards. Funny that my people should be ever falling farther behind. The more they try to imitate whites, the more tragic the result. Yet they want us to be imitation white men. About all we imitate well are their vices.

The village is not a sight to instill pride, yet I am not ashamed. One can never be ashamed of his own people when he knows they have dreams as beautiful as white snow on a tall pine.

Father and my brother and sister are seated around the table as I walk in. Father stares at me for a moment. Then I am in his arms, crying on his shoulder. I give them the presents I have brought, and my throat tightens as I watch my sister

American Indians, also known as Native Americans, were the first people known to live on the North American continent. Unfortunately, with the coming of the Europeans beginning in the fifteenth century, the American Indians gradually lost most of their lands and their way of life. Although pieces of land called "reservations" were set aside for them, many could not survive the poor conditions in which they found themselves.

sprawled: Spread out in a disordered way.
pulse: Heartbeat.
etched: Formed as though their outlines have been cut into the sky with a sharp instrument. "... black in the night" is a clue.
vices: Here it means bad habits.
instill: Firmly establish.

save carefully bits of red string from the packages. I hide my feelings by wrestling with my brother when he strikes my shoulder in a token of affection. Father looks at me, and I know he has many questions, but he seems to know why I have come. He tells me to go on alone to the lodge, and he will follow.

I walk along the trail to the lodge, watching the northern lights forming in the heavens. White waving ribbons that seem to pulsate with the rhythm of the drums. Clean snow creaks beneath my feet, and a soft wind sighs through the trees, singing to me. Everything seems to say, "Be happy! You are home now—you are free. You are among friends—we are your friends; we, the trees, and the snow, and the lights."

I follow the trail to the lodge. My feet are light, my heart seems to sing to the music, and I hold my head high. Across white snow fields blue winds are dancing.

Before the lodge door I stop, afraid. I wonder if my people will remember me. I wonder—"Am I Indian, or am I white?" I stand before the door a long time. I hear the ice groan on the lake, and remember the story of the old woman who is under the ice, trying to get out, so she can punish some runaway lovers. I think to myself, "If I am white, I will not believe that story. If I am Indian, I will know that there is an old woman under the ice." I listen for a while, and I know that there is an old woman under the ice. I look again at the lights and go in.

Inside the lodge there are many Indians. Some sit on benches around the walls. Others dance in the center of the floor around a drum. Nobody seems to notice me. It seems as though I were among a people I have never seen before. Heavy women with long black hair. Women with children on their knees—small children that watch with intent black eyes the movements of

wrestling: *Struggling or fighting in close body contact in an effort to bring another to the floor.*
token: *A small sample standing for the whole thing.*
lodge: *Here it means a building in which American Indian religious ceremonies are often held.*

pulsate: *Move to a strong beat (*puls- *means to beat).*
" *. . . the rhythm of the drums" is a clue.*
creaks: *Makes a squeaking sound.*
groan: *Make a moaning sound.*

the dancers, whose small faces are solemn and serene.

The faces of the old people are serene, too, and their eyes are merry and bright. I look at the old men. Straight, dressed in dark trousers and beaded velvet vests, wearing soft moccasins. Dark, lined faces intent on the music. I wonder if I am at all like them. They dance on, lifting their feet to the rhythm of the drums, swaying lightly, looking upward. I look at their eyes and am startled at the rapt attention to the rhythm of the music.

The dance stops. The men walk back to the walls and talk in low tones or with their hands. There is little conversation, yet everyone seems to be sharing some secret. A woman looks at a small boy wandering away, and he comes back to her.

Strange, I think, and then remember. These people are not sharing words—they are sharing a mood. Everyone is happy. I am so used to white people that it seems strange so many people could be together without someone talking. These Indians are happy because they are together, and because the night is beautiful outside, and the music is beautiful.

I try hard to forget school and white people, and be one of these—my people. I try to forget everything but the night, and it is a part of me; that I am one with my people and we are all a part of something universal. I watch eyes and see now that the old people are speaking to me. They nod slightly, imperceptibly, and their eyes laugh into mine. I look around the room. All the eyes are friendly; they all laugh. No one questions my being here. The drums begin to beat again, and I catch the invitation in the eyes of the old men. My feet begin to lift to the rhythm, and I look out beyond the walls into the night and see the lights. I am happy. It is beautiful. I am home.

Thinking about Your Prereading Reactions

Return to the paragraphs on page 19. Think again about your answers to the questions. How close did Thomas Whitecloud's experience come to what you thought it would be like to return home?

Understanding Intended Meaning

Discuss the following questions with your class.

1. What does Thomas Whitecloud mean when he says, "I am alone—alone but not nearly so lonely as I was back on the campus at school"? Why does he feel more lonely when surrounded by people than he does when physically alone in the snow and the pines? Have you ever felt this way? Explain.

2. What mixed feelings does Thomas have about going to be with his people at the lodge? How do you know?

---

solemn: Very serious.
serene: Calm.
trousers: The British word for pants.
beaded: Covered with beads.
moccasins: Leather slippers traditionally made and worn by

American Indians.
swaying: Moving back and forth in a swinging motion.
rapt: Completely involved.
imperceptibly: Not noticeably (here im- means not; -percept- refers to noticeable). "They nod slightly" is a clue.

3. The Indians at the lodge at first appear to ignore Thomas. What do you think is happening? Do you think that they, too, might have mixed feelings about his returning? Explain.

4. Why do you think Thomas's throat tightens as he watches his sister save the red string from his gifts? What does this action tell you about the family's economic situation?

5. What do you think Thomas means when he says, "I am one with my people and we are all a part of something universal"? Do you think we are all a part of something universal? Explain.

6. What do you think finally brings Thomas back into his people's world?

Determining the Main Idea

The main idea of a story is the most important idea that the author is trying to express. Which of the following statements comes closest to expressing the main idea of "Blue Winds Dancing"?

- ◆ One should never be ashamed of one's own people and their way of life.
- ◆ The American Indians often lead difficult lives in the United States.
- ◆ Going back home can be a joyful experience, but it often has its moments of fear and tension.
- ◆ People always know deep inside if they still belong to their first culture and the people who are part of it.
- ◆ Going back to nature is one of the best things a person can do.

Discuss your answer with your class and the teacher.

Now read the story again before proceeding to the following activities. This time you may want to examine more carefully any details you did not fully understand during your first reading.

Finding Information to Support Conclusions

It is important to be able to support conclusions or decisions that we make. The conclusions below are about Thomas Whitecloud. Find a few details from the story to support each one.

Conclusion 1: Thomas Whitecloud is happy to be back with nature.

Supporting Details:

Example: He laughs as he goes into the woods.

I know there are the tracks of deer and rabbits... feeling glad

I watch him and am glad.

My feet are light, my heart seem to sing to the music

Conclusion 2: Thomas Whitecloud knows he is Indian and not white.

Supporting Details:

He believes "an old man under ice.

Yet, they want us to be imitation white men.

I am one of my people

I am home.

Compare your work with that of one or more of your classmates. Make any changes that seem necessary.

Comparing Cultural Expectations

Stories generally mean much more to us if we can relate them to our own cultural backgrounds. Discuss two or more of the following questions about culture with a small group.

1. Think about the statement "I am back in a world where time does not mean so much now" (page 20). Discuss how the culture you know best looks at time.

2. We learned that Thomas Whitecloud places great value on being with nature. How important is nature in the culture you know best?

3. Think about the statement "I hide my feelings by wrestling with my brother when he strikes my shoulder in a token of affection" (page 22). In what ways is affection shown in the culture you know best? Consider a few of the following relationships. How do these people show affection for each other?

   love

   ◆ husband/wife
   ◆ brother/sister
   ◆ brother/brother
   ◆ sister/sister
   ◆ daughter/mother
   ◆ son/mother
   ◆ daughter/father
   ◆ son/father

4. At the lodge Thomas reflects, "I am so used to white people that it seems strange so many people could be together without someone talking" (page 23). Are there other societies where this is also true? Is this trait good or bad, in your opinion?

5. What do you think Thomas means when he says, "The more they [the Indians] try to imitate whites, the more tragic the result. Yet they want us to be imitation white men. About all we imitate well are their vices" (page 21)? Are you familiar with similar tragedies that have happened in other places? Why do such tragedies occur? What can be done to prevent them?

imitate : bắt chước

Appreciating Descriptive Language

Descriptive language brings literature alive for the reader. It sometimes involves comparisons in which objects or ideas are given human qualities. This kind of comparison is called *personification.* Thomas Whitecloud uses personification in the title "Blue Winds Dancing" (as though winds could dance as a person might) and in the story when he says "the pines are *wearing* white shawls" (page 20). Find other examples of personification in the story and write them on the lines below. Underline the words that are usually used to describe humans.

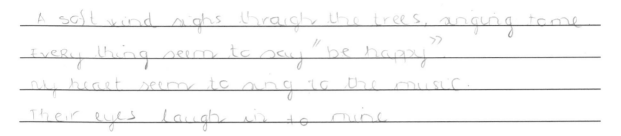

A soft wind sighs through the trees, singing to me

Every thing seem to say "be happy"

my heart seem to sing to the music.

Their eyes laugh in to mine

Does personification help you to enjoy and appreciate the story? If so, in what ways? Discuss your opinions with your class.

Developing Your Word Bank

Many of the more common words and phrases used in this unit reappear in other selections throughout the book. List in your Word Bank (see page 152) a few of the words or phrases that are new to you. Choose only those items that you feel will be useful. You may want to work with a partner or have your teacher help you with this task. Consider words you might want to use in conversation, in writing, or in communication about an academic area in which you have a special interest.

Ideas for Discussion and/or Writing

Choose one or more of the following activities.

1. Write a letter to Thomas Whitecloud. In your letter, tell him what you like about his village and its people.

2. Discuss the quote "a gift is a gift, if a man buys it with his last quarter" (page 20). Think about the meaning of gift giving and the kinds of gifts that you like to give and receive.

3. In the library, find as much information as you can about a particular tribe of American Indians. Take a look at its history, its culture, and problems in the United States. Your teacher or the librarian may be able to help you in your search. Share the information you find with a small group.

4. Thomas Whitecloud says he likes to "watch houses and try to imagine what might be happening in them" (page 20). Look again at the picture of a house on page 18. Write a story about the people you think might be living there. Let your imagination be your guide. When you are finished, share your writing with a partner. Ask your partner questions about it. Does your partner understand it? Are the characters interesting? Do they seem like real people? Is what happens in the story believable to you as a reader? You and your classmates might want to put your stories together in a book to share with others.

5. Find a partner. One of you can take the part of the Indian who returns home in "Blue Winds Dancing" while the other takes the part of one of the older Indians at the lodge. Make up a dialogue, write it down, and practice it. Then share your scene with the class.

LETTING GO

How can I leave you behind, my friend?
You who have been in my heart so long . . .

Life often requires people to let go of something. It could be an old car that costs too much to keep running or a boat for which you no longer have room. It could be an idea you hold dear or a way of behaving that no longer works. Or it could be something very special from the culture you know best. What are a few of the things you have had to give up over the years? How did giving them up make you feel? In what ways were you able to adjust to the change? Discuss with a partner.

Howard Maier, the author of the following story, has been called into the United States Army during World War II. He finds that the most difficult thing he must let go of is a living thing—his dog Spook. In the author's eyes, Spook is a rare treasure. He is a beautiful Irish setter, a dog with long hair and a reddish copper coat. After much agony, the author finally asks an old friend, a garage owner in upstate New York, to take care of his beloved animal. . . .

from The Red Dog

Howard Maier

Yes, my friend said, he would take him and hunt him and care for him. But he said nothing about love; for though men may write this word, they rarely use it. I watched him as he patted the dog's head and the hand was gentle, and Spook thumped the floor with his tail, but his eyes remained fixed on my face.

All the way up in the car he had watched me instead of hanging himself half out of the window in his customary manner; a dog senses many things besides game. Without another word, I handed my friend the lead and got into my car and drove away; and even today I cannot truly remember whether I heard Spook bark or I only imagined it. Generally I am a slow and careful driver; but that day I drove for ten miles at top speed before slowing down.

After a month in the army I wrote my friend a letter inquiring about the dog. I received no reply. Each camp was farther afield and from each camp I wrote a letter. No answer ever came. I began to write to other friends in the village; and in each letter I asked for news of my dog. Some of them answered—but of those that did, none spoke of the dog. Spook is dead, I

thought. He must be—otherwise they would answer. Rather than face the actuality of it, I gave up making inquiries and tried my best to put the dog from my mind.

Four years passed; the war was over. I had married and my wife and I lived in the city. Summer was here and we had taken a small house in the upstate village for our vacation. As we packed the bags in the car, Laurette suddenly looked up and said, "Suppose we run into your Spook?"

"Spook is dead," I said; she took one look at my face and never finished her question.

The minute we arrived at the village I drove to the garage although the tank was still half full. I left Laurette in the car and went into the office. My friend greeted me is if only a weekend had intervened since our last meeting, as if there had been no war, as if there had never been a question of a dog between us. Finally I couldn't stand it any longer and blurted out, "What happened to Spook?"

"Why nothing happened to him," my friend said. "He's as hale and hearty as you or I. I saw him only the other day."

---

upstate: *The northern part of the state.*
hunt him: *Here it means take him hunting.*
customary: *Usual.*
game: *The animals that are killed by hunters.*
lead: *The British word for leash (the leather strap or rope used to control a dog).*
inquiring: *Asking (-quir- refers to asking). ". . . about the dog" is a clue.*

afield: *Away. ". . . farther" is a clue.*
face the actuality: *Accept as fact. "I gave up making inquiries" is a clue.*
intervened: *Here it means came between two points of time (inter- means between; -ven- means to come). ". . . since our last meeting" is a clue.*
blurted out: *Said quickly without thought. "Finally I couldn't stand it any longer" is a clue.*
hale and hearty: *An old-fashioned way to say healthy.*

quản cứu viên, sứ giản nhé

duyên dạng

My relief was so sharp that there was no room for anger. Bewildered, I asked, "What do you mean you saw him? Don't you have him anymore?"

At that he had the grace to look shamefaced. He said, "I was drafted, and I didn't know I was going to be turned down, so I gave him away to a minister, lives up above Willow."

"Why didn't you answer my letter?"

His face flushed with embarrassment. "I'm no hand at writing," he said. "Don't think I've written a letter in ten years."

I stared at him. Was it possible that he, having read my letters pleading for news of the dog, didn't realize what Spook meant to me?

The fact that he didn't was written on his honest, embarrassed face. He was country-bred. To him a dog was an animal; it slept outdoors with the other animals and when fall came it was hunted, and that was all.

"What's the name of the minister?" I asked him.

"Oh, Spook's not with him anymore. To tell the truth, he's had five, maybe six masters since then. Lives up with some summer people named Crocker now, up past Shady. He's a valley dog now."

"A valley dog?"

"On his own. Cruises back and forth. Twenty miles one way or the other's nothing to him. Perfect condition, hard as nails. In the fall a man goes out with a gun and there's Spook ready and willing to tag along."

lõ rảng

There was nothing to say; it was obvious that he thought the life of a valley dog the best possible life any dog could have.

"Sorry about the letter," he said, still ashamed. *xấu hổ*

"It's all right." I paid for my gas and went out to the car. I drove the mile to the house without saying anything. All the way Laurette kept looking at me. When we turned into the drive, she said gently, "Spook's alive, isn't he?"

I nodded my head and we let it go at that. After dinner I told her the whole story and she let me tell it without asking any questions. At the end, she asked, "Are you going to try to see him?"

"Well sure," I said. "Why not?"

"I wouldn't," Laurette said. "It would only hurt you, and it would hurt him more. Don't try to find him; it sounds as if he's very happy now."

"Don't be silly. Do you think he'll remember me? After four years and six masters?"

She just looked at me and that was the end of the discussion. Two weeks passed and we worked and went swimming and lay around and we never talked about the dog.

Then one day I saw Spook.

During a climb up the side of the valley I had stopped to rest on a rock which overlooked an open pasture in the woods beneath us. A boy of about sixteen came out of the trees, and then a second later Spook raced out into the sunlight. I knew him at once. I would have known Spook anywhere.

The boy walked straight across the pasture; but Spook, as was his habit, quartered the fields, racing far ahead, then back again. . . . I had seldom seen him look so well or so beautiful. It took them about three minutes to cross the field; then the trees on the far side swallowed them both. The pasture had never been so empty.

When I returned to the house I told Laurette about it. She said, "Away up there on the side of the hill—how could you know it was Spook?"

"How do I know you're you?"

---

bewildered: Puzzled. "What do you mean you saw him? Don't you have him any more?" is a clue.
I'm no hand at writing: I'm not a very good writer.
country-bred: Raised in the country.
cruises: Travels. ". . . back and forth" is a clue.

tag along: Go along with or follow.
let it go at that: Didn't continue with a discussion or thought.
pasture: An open field upon which grow grasses and other plants eaten by grazing animals.
quartered: Divided something into four equal parts.

The next time I saw Spook, Laurette was with me. It was night, during one of those heavy summer rainstorms that come up so suddenly. We were having dinner on the covered terrace of the local restaurant. Padding up the street came a dog, head down, tail down, looking as miserable as only an Irish setter can when it's soaking wet. As the dog came into the light cast by the terrace lamps, I said, "That looks like Spook." I must have pronounced the name quite loudly, for the dog stopped and his head came up. It was Spook.

He pushed in the screen door, walked across the flagged terrace, water dripping from his matted coat, and came up to my side. He stood there looking into my face for a minute, then—without a bark or a wag of his tail—curled up on the stone at my feet. He dropped his head on his paws, but never once closed his eyes; he watched every move I made, just the way he used to. Four years, four long years, I thought, and felt all sort of choked up. The waitress brought our food; at the sight of the wet dog, she said, "Here you . . ."

"Let him be!" I said, so sharply that the

woman was startled. Laurette explained to her. Once during the meal I got up to go into the dining room. Spook got up and went with me, all the way there and back, his head so close to my leg that my trousers brushed against him.

When we left the restaurant, Spook followed us; when I opened the door of the car, he was first in, over the front seat, and into his accustomed place in the right-hand back corner, his head pressed against the window.

"What are you going to do?" Laurette asked me.

"What can I do on a night like this?" I asked. She nodded her head understandingly.

"Let's go home, then."

We took Spook back to the little house with us. The open fire dried out his coat and the feathers on his legs got all curly and blonde. He lay there on the floor between Laurette's chair and my desk, his head toward me. If I stood up, he was instantly on his feet. At about ten o'clock, exactly as he had always done, he came over to my chair, placed a paw on my knee, cocked his head to one side and gazed silently into my face.

---

terrace: *A platform forming a type of porch or patio.*
padding: *Walking with soft steps. "... head down, tail down" is a clue.*
flagged: *Made of flagstone, which is a flat stone split into pieces and used to make a cover over the ground.*

choked up: *Ready to cry.*
accustomed: *Customary.*
cocked: *Tilted or turned up. "... to one side" is a clue.*
gazed: *Stared.*

"What does he want?" Laurette asked.

"Out," I said, and I got up and opened the screen door for him. The rain had stopped and the moon had risen. Staring out into the darkness which had swallowed up the dog, I said over my shoulder, "Well, that's that, I guess. He'll go home now, to wherever home is." And for an instant I was filled with regret that I had so sternly held myself back from touching him or even so much as speaking to him in the old intimate way.

Back at the desk I couldn't work. I stared at the blank paper in my typewriter. The paper didn't even exist for me, nor the room—not even Laurette existed for me. I was caught in the world outside the house; my ears strained for the slightest whisper or rustle in the grass.

At about eleven, two quick imperious barks sounded outside the screen door. Laurette lifted her eyebrows inquiringly.

"He wants in," I told her. I jumped up from my chair and stood there helplessly in the center of the room, not knowing what to do.

"Well, go on, let him in," she said. "We'll talk later."

So I let him in, and when we went to bed he took his usual position on the floor beside my bed. I could hear him there, breathing softly in the darkness. Laurette talked to me.

"This is why I didn't want you to see him again," she said.

"But he was only two years old when I left him, and after four years, who would believe he's remembered me this way?" His act of remembrance had been with me all right. It was a wonderful thing.

"It's just as if I had never gone away," I said.

"Try not to think of that," Laurette said.

"Think of Spook. Think how beautiful and fit he is, and remember that he's leading the proper life for a dog. A whole valley to roam in. What kind of life would he lead with us in the big city?" With both of us working, what could he have? A walk on a lead twice a day? Never any grass, or any sun—never to run free. You wouldn't want to take him back to that, now that he's had the other, would you?"

"But I'm not doing anything," I protested. "I haven't even petted him. He's doing it all himself."

"The decision is up to you. You have to make it."

"All right, then," I said. "We'll take him back to the Crockers tomorrow."

She reached across and patted my arm and said no more. I don't know how long it took me to get to sleep that night. All I remember now is that once during the night I heard Spook get up and change position; I heard him hit the floor with a thud the way setters do. As he stretched out again I heard him sigh, a sound that seemed to contain all the contentment in the world.

We started for the Crockers' place at noon the next day. It was blazing hot. We drove the five miles in complete silence, except for Spook, who occasionally would whine anxiously deep in his throat.

We turned off the road and up the lane and circled the drive of the big house. When I took Spook out of the car, my fingers were tight about his collar: he was whining continually, and nothing in the world could have made me look into his eyes.

The boy I had seen in the pasture that other morning answered my knock; he looked

---

regret: A feeling of grief and sorrow.
intimate: Familiar or close.
strained: Used great effort to hear. "... for the slightest whisper" is a clue.
rustle: A whispering sound. "... in the grass" is a clue.
imperious: Urgent or commanding (imperi- refers to an empire).
protested: Strongly objected.

contentment: The state of being satisfied or content.
blazing: Extremely and intensely hot (blaze means to burn like a hot flame).
whine: Give out a high-pitched cry.

astounded at seeing me with the dog. And all the time I talked to him, explaining what had happened, Spook kept pulling to break my hold on his collar. At last the boy understood the situation and took hold of Spook's collar, and I got back in the car and drove off.

We had gone only about a mile on the macadam when I saw him in the rear-view mirror. He was racing after the car, running his heart out.

"That fool kid let him loose!" I said, and put on the speed, but I couldn't tear my eyes from the mirror. He kept running and running, and the sun kept beating down on him, and I knew he would never give up. Suddenly Laurette said in a tense voice, "Do you want to kill him? Stop the car. Stop the car, do you hear?"

Pulling off the road and onto the grass, I got out of the car and waited. Spook came up and sank exhausted at my feet, his chest laboring painfully, his tongue hanging from his mouth. There was a little sound from the car and I turned around. Laurette was crying softly, the tears running down her cheeks.

"Spook, poor Spook," she kept saying through her sobs. "Don't worry anymore, not anymore please. We'll take him with us. It'll be all right, fine. You can walk him in the morning before you go to work, and I'll come home on my lunch hour and take him then. And Bessy won't mind taking him out once in the afternoon." Bessy was our maid. "We'll manage somehow," Laurette said.

I patted her shoulder and gave her my handkerchief. I put Spook back in the car and turned it around and headed back for the Crocker place. Laurette put a restraining hand on my arm.

"No dear," I said. "It wouldn't work. Last night you talked with your head; now you're talking with your heart. Believe me, the head's better."

This time I told the boy to lock Spook in the house and when we drove away, I drove very fast and Laurette said nothing about the speed.

All this took place more than three years ago. Today I rarely think of Spook, consciously anyway. But three or four times every year, I have a recurring dream, a horrible nightmare.

The scene of the dream is always the same; at the stretch of macadam highway. I am myself, in the car, and at the same time I am Spook—and I run and run and the car never stops, and the hard, cruel road hits my paws and the sun beatsdown on me and I keep saying over and over again: He doesn't want me, he doesn't want me and then I feel a grief so sharp that I cannot

---

astounded: Amazed.
macadam: A highway made of layers of small stones and tar.
running his heart out: Running as fast as possible, with all his energy.
laboring: Working with great effort. ". . . his tongue hanging from his mouth" is a clue.

restraining: Holding back.
recurring: Happening again and again (re- means back; -curr- means run). ". . . three or four times every year" is a clue.

contain it, and my heart swells and swells and threatens to burst with the sheer pity of it. At this point I always wake up in a cold sweat and I slip quietly out of bed, for I have never told Laurette about the recurring dream.

I go into the living room and light a cigarette and stare out of the window. The streets are empty; the dark, cold stone houses hem them in. There are no trees, and that helps. I force myself to remember Spook as I saw him that day in the green pasture running free, with the soft grass beneath his feet and the wind whipping his ears back and the sun striking from his gleaming copper coat. That helps, too.

I put out my cigarette and go back to bed and to sleep. But even now, three years later, even now after writing it all down, I do not know whether the decision I made for Spook was right or wrong.

Thinking about Your Prereading Reactions

Return to the paragraph on page 30. Think again about your own experiences with letting go. How close did the experiences of the author come to your own?

Understanding Intended Meaning

Discuss the following questions with your class.

1. What makes the author think his dog is dead?

2. What has really happened to the dog while the author has been gone?

3. Does the author try to see his dog when he returns? What happens?

4. When the author tells Laurette that he has seen Spook, she says, "Away up there on the side of the hill—how could you know it was Spook?" He replies, "How do I know you're you?" (page 32). What does this tell you about the author's relationship with his dog?

5. The author is filled with regret to have been so stern with the dog (see page 34). Why do you think he feels this way?

6. Describe the author's recurring dream.

7. How does the author comfort himself?

Now read the story again before proceeding to the following activities. This time you may want to examine more carefully any details you did not fully understand during your first reading.

---

contain: Here it means to hold something inside (con- *means together;* -tain *refers to holding).*

sheer: Here it means not mixed with anything; pure.

Identify the Setting

The setting of a story is where the story takes place. Where does this story take place? Is the setting itself important to the meaning of the story? If so, in what way? Discuss your answers with your class.

Tracking the Plot of the Story

The plot of a story consists of the chain of events that occur (see the example chain which follows). Each link in the chain represents an event that is important to the meaning of the story. The following chain is begun for you. Finish the chain, adding more links if you need them. Make sure you include only the most important happenings in the story.

Chain of Events

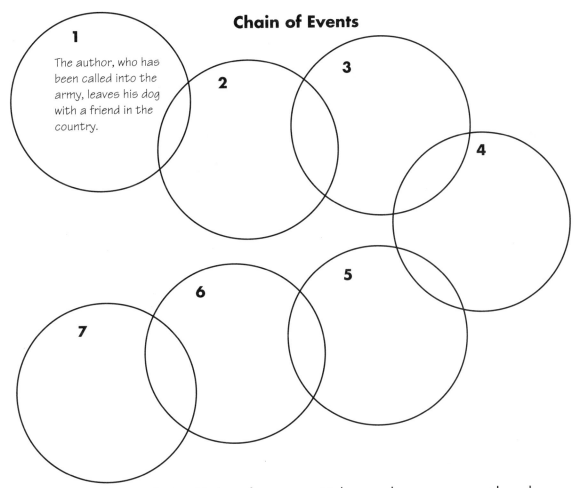

1 The author, who has been called into the army, leaves his dog with a friend in the country.

2

3

4

5

6

7

Compare your chain with that of a partner. Make any changes you want based on what you learn.

Comparing Cultural Expectations

Discuss one or both of the following questions with a small group.

1. The author reports that his friend said nothing about love for Spook. The author goes on to say, "for though men may write this word, they rarely use it" (page 31). Is the word love avoided by men in the cultures you know best? What about by women? Explain.

2. When talking about his friend later in the story, the author concludes, "To him a dog was an animal; it slept outdoors with the other animals and when fall came it was hunted, and that was all" (page 32). Is this attitude toward pets common in the cultures you know best? Explain.

Relating to Self

Discuss one or more of the following questions with a partner.

1. When the author decides that he wants to find his dog, Laurette, his wife, says, "I wouldn't. It would only hurt you, and it would hurt him more. Don't try to find him; it sounds as if he's very happy now" (page 32). Do you feel this was good or bad advice? If the dog had been your animal, would you have taken such advice? Why or why not?

2. Do you think the author's final decision to leave the dog with its country owners was right or wrong? Would you have been able to do what the author did? Have you ever had to make a similar decision concerning a pet? Explain.

3. When Laurette decides that they should keep the dog after it runs after the car, the author replies, "No dear. It wouldn't work. Last night you talked with your head; now you're talking with your heart. Believe me, the head's better" (page 35). What does he mean? From your own experience, is it better to talk with your heart or with your head? Explain.

The following story is about the daughter of Norwegian immigrants living in northern Minnesota. She led a good life with her husband Elmer up until his death. Now letting go for her means leaving her home for a while. But there are other things that she also has trouble giving up. . . .

Leaving Home

Wendy Abbott Hansen

Sharon raced to the phone and answered it on the fifth ring. "Hello," she panted out of breath.

"Ya,[1] well I was just going through Elmer's things as I was packing for my trip to Cannon Falls,[2] and I felt kind of down in the dumps," Ella's voice broke off.

Ella was going to live with her brother Gustav and his wife in southern Minnesota for the winter months, as she had done for several years. She could no longer heat her home properly with her kitchen wood stove. Arthritis in her knees and feet made the trip to the wood pile an impossible task in snow and ice.

"It must be pretty lonesome for you now, Ella, living without him," Sharon replied. She noticed that Ella's voice had been soft and low, not her usual tone which always sounded like yelling even though she wasn't angry. Sharon felt the pang of the emptiness Ella must feel living in that cluttered cabin all alone and preparing for her winter pilgrimage alone. "Why don't you have supper with us tonight, Ella?" asked Sharon.

"Oh that is so much driving for you, Sharon," said Ella.

"Martin and Donny will be glad to know you're coming. I'll pick you up at 5:00," said Sharon.

When Sharon went to get her, Ella had on her brown scarf tied under her chin which made her look like a quaint woman of the old country. Her heavy black shoes and house dress from the 50s completed the look.

"Ya, I'm just getting packed now for the winter—never mind this mess," she said.

Sharon looked around the three-room cabin. Piles of clothes in plastic bags were stacked on chairs, the kitchen table and counters. She looked into the bedroom where Ella slept and saw the unmade bed with piles of shoes and stockings on top. The living room contained small

---

down in the dumps: *Depressed.*
arthritis: *A painful swelling in the joints of the body. ". . . made the trip to the wood pile an impossible task" is a clue.*
pang: *A sudden, intense feeling or rush of emotion.*
cluttered: *Filled with things in an unorganized way.*

pilgrimage: *A journey for an important, sometimes sacred, purpose (a pilgrim is a traveler).*
quaint: *Old-fashioned in a pleasing way.*
the old country: *The country from which one's ancestors came. Here it means Norway.*

pathways to walk between mountains of magazines, books and boxes. "Actually," thought Sharon, "it doesn't look very different than it usually does."

The years of collecting things that would never be used but could not be thrown away had crowded Ella and Elmer into a smaller and smaller living space.

"There's the neighbors' flowers I rescued last night from that cold north wind we had," said Ella. "She must have paid good money for that plant," she continued, pointing to a pot of red geraniums.

Sharon marveled at the careful attention Ella paid to the flowers amidst her household of benign neglect.

"I'll bring my flashlight so I can see my way in the dark," said Ella.

It occurred to Sharon that Ella would not consider turning her outside house light on to leave it lit while she was gone. "Old habits formed in lean years are not easily shed," she thought.

"Ella looks smaller in my house and a little lost," thought Sharon as they all sat together at Sharon's kitchen table.

Sharon could not think of why she felt such contentment at having Ella in her home. Ella's long hair braided and coiled, her faded house dress and black rubber overshoes gave Sharon such a safe and sad feeling all at once.

The supper discussion centered around Elmer and Ella's life together on the shore of Lake Superior.[3] Elmer had been a fisherman all his life. First as a young man in Norway and later on the North Shore of Lake Superior. Ella, born of Norwegian immigrants, grew up in a large farm family and was used to daily bread

baking and meal preparation for the family and hired hands. Their years of hard work and struggle gave them both a no-nonsense, practical view of the world. Sharon recalled the single rose draped over Elmer's homemade casket at the funeral. He had arranged ahead of time for Sharon's husband to build the simple, pine casket in order to save Ella the funeral expenses.

Ella, spying Sharon's stove, said she had never used an electric stove and wouldn't even know how to use one.

"Always I have cooked and baked with my wood stove," she said. "Every morning I was the first one up and I fired the stove with the pieces of wood I had drying in the oven. Then I made the coffee and listened to the news and weather on the radio. When the coffee was ready and the room warm, Elmer would get out of bed and we would eat our oatmeal with a little brown sugar. Now when I wake up, I often forget that Elmer is not there waiting for his coffee," she said.

The waves crashed on the frozen shore as Sharon walked alongside Ella. The pathway to Ella's house was narrow and they had to shine the flashlight at their feet to avoid the slippery rocks. Thinking of the cold cabin Ella was returning to, Sharon said, "Are you glad to be going to your brother's house where you will be warm and cozy this winter?"

"Ya, you know it is all right there, but it is not my home," she replied.

She turned her outside house light on for Sharon to see her way back to the car. "See you in the spring," said Sharon.

"Ya, I'll be home in the spring," said Ella.

---

geraniums: A type of plant with brightly colored flowers and divided leaves.
benign: Harmless (beni- refers to well).
lean years: Years when there is not much money to provide the necessities of living.

shed: Here is means gotten rid of.
coiled: Arranged in a circle.
hired hands: People who are paid for work that they usually do with their hands.

Understanding Intended Meaning

Discuss the following questions with your class.

1. What is Ella's mood when she calls Sharon on the phone?

2. How does Sharon react to her friend? What invitation does she give?

3. Briefly describe the life that Ella and her husband Elmer led while he was alive.

4. Where is Ella planning to go? How does she feel about leaving?

Making Inferences

Often the reader is expected to infer meaning or draw his or her own conclusions about a story based on details or clues presented by the author. Discuss the following with a small group.

1. Throughout the story, there are hints that Ella is having difficulty letting go. Consider the following facts from the story. Does each appear to involve a difficulty with letting go? Explain.

   a. Ella is depressed while going through her husband's things.

   b. Ella can no longer heat her home properly with her kitchen wood stove.

   c. Ella has a brown scarf tied under her chin, which makes her look like a quaint woman of the old country.

   d. Ella had collected "things that would never be used but could not be thrown away" (page 40).

   e. Ella will not consider leaving her outside house light lit while she is gone.

2. Why does Sharon feel content when Ella is in her home? Why might Ella's "long hair braided and coiled, her faded house dress and black rubber overshoes" give Sharon "a safe and sad feeling all at once" (page 40)?

3. What does the simple funeral tell you about Ella and her life-style? What things does she consider important in life? In other words, what are her values?

Relating to Self

Discuss one or both of the following questions with a partner.

1. Do you have a friend or frequent guest whose presence brings you contentment? If so, describe that person. Why do you feel content when he or she is around? Is that person similar to Ella in any ways?

2. If you have moved from one culture to another, what parts of your first culture were the most difficult to let go? Consider people, customs, foods, activities, and other things that you have not been able to include in your new life. Was there anything in your new culture that gave you comfort and helped you to deal with and adjust to the situation? If you have never made a move to a new culture, consider what you think might be most difficult for you to give up.

Identifying the Point of View

A story is usually told from the point of view of the author, one of the characters, or some omniscient (all-knowing) being. Generally, a story is told in the first person *I* or in the third person *he, she,* or *it.*

From which point of view is "The Red Dog" told? From which point of view is "Leaving Home" told? Do you think the point of view made any difference in your enjoyment of either story? Discuss your answers with your class and the teacher.

Developing Your Word Bank

Many of the more common words and phrases used in this unit reappear in other selections throughout the book. List in your Word Bank (see page 152) a few of the words or phrases that are new to you. Choose only those items that you feel will be useful. You may want to work with a partner or have your teacher help you with this task. Consider words you might want to use in conversation, in writing, or in communication about an academic area in which you have a special interest.

Ideas for Discussion and/or Writing

Choose one or more of the following activities.

1. Write your own story about someone who has had to let go of something dear. Use the first person *I* or the third person *he* or *she*. Your class may want to make a collection of stories to share with others.

2. There are many kinds of attachments or things that are hard to let go of other than those discussed in this unit. Talk about some of them with a small group. Consider not only attachments that may be good but also those that may be harmful or even dangerous (for example, attachments to drugs or to people who are not positive forces in your life). After your discussion, choose one kind of attachment and write about it. You may want to find information in your library about your topic (your teacher or the librarian may be able to help you in your search). You will probably want to include personal experience and/or the experiences of others. Share your writing with a partner. Ask your partner questions such as: Did I state my ideas clearly? What do you understand my ideas to be? Do you agree? Why or why not?

3. One subject that was mentioned in "The Red Dog" but was not discussed is the topic of hunting for sport. In the United States, hunting for sport is a very controversial issue. Some people feel that hunting for sport is cruel. Moreover, they feel that it threatens the populations of some animals who may be in danger of disappearing forever. Other people feel that hunting is a basic right of humans and that it is healthy recreation, especially for those living in noisy, crowded cities. It gives such people a chance to be out in nature. How do you feel about hunting? How strong are your feelings? You may want to have a debate or formal discussion with your classmates on the subject.

4. The story "Leaving Home" contains this saying: "Old habits formed in lean years are not easily shed" (page 40). With a small group, discuss the meaning of this sentence. Can you and your group think of other sayings that have similar meanings? Consider, for example, "You can't teach an old dog new tricks" or "A leopard can't change its spots." Make a list of such sayings. Include as many from other cultures as you can. Discuss to what extent you think the sayings may be true.

Notes
1. *Ya* is a commonly used shortened form of yes. The Norwegian word for yes (*ja*) is very similar.
2. Cannon Falls is a town in southern Minnesota.
3. Lake Superior is located in the northern United States and is part of the Great Lakes chain.

UNIT 4
ALL THAT GLITTERS

Carmel Point

*Margaret Phyllis
MacSweeney*

I watched a sea anemone
The color of green jade
Shadowed under water.

I saw a daring crab,
Unafraid and young
Touch the velvet petals
Of that princess under water.
Softly she took him in,
Softly she sighed and closed.
The little crab was hushed and still—
Never would he swim again
Under crevice, under weed,
Under green and colored water.

Softly she opened—
That princess of rare jade
Softly she gave him back
Sucked of all his pearly flesh
Sucked of all his salty blood. . . .

Discuss these questions with your class. What happened to the crab in the above poem? Might something similar happen to humans? Think about people who, like the crab, are attracted to something dangerous.

Now look at the title of this unit— "All That Glitters." The words are from a well-known proverb. A proverb is a popular statement of belief about a common experience. The complete proverb from which the title comes is "All that glitters is not gold." What do you think this proverb means? Do you think the poem and the proverb are saying a similar thing? If so, what is their message?

sea anemone: (pronounced " ə-nĕm´-ə-nē ") A very brightly colored, flowerlike animal that sits at the bottom of the sea. It has thin arms or tentacles that sway invitingly around its large hidden mouth.

crevice: A narrow opening or crack (crev- refers to a crack or split).
jade: A gemstone that is usually green.

from **The Pearl**

John Steinbeck

Kino, a fisherman near La Paz, Mexico, has found a great pearl at the bottom of the sea. He imagines that it will bring him wealth and happiness such as he has never known before. At last he will be able to give his wife Juana and his tiny baby Coyotito the things poverty could never buy them. However, evil men have plans of their own for the pearl, and they will stop at nothing, even murder, to get it. As this part of the story begins, Kino and his family have left their village in the night, only to find themselves in the desert and in even greater danger as they continue to struggle against the forces of evil.

. . . The sun had passed over the stone mountains when Kino and Juana struggled up the steep broken slope and came at last to the water. From this step they could look out over the sunbeaten desert to the blue Gulf in the distance. They came utterly weary to the pool, and Juana slumped to her knees and first washed Coyotito's face and then filled her bottle and gave him a drink. And the baby was weary and petulant, and he cried softly until Juana gave him her breast, and then he gurgled and clucked against her. Kino drank long and thirstily at the pool. For a moment, then, he stretched out beside the water and relaxed all his muscles and watched Juana feeding the baby, and then he got to his feet and went to the edge of the step where the water slipped over, and he searched the distance carefully. His eyes set on a point and he became rigid. Far down the slope he could see the two trackers; they were little more than dots or scurrying ants and behind them a larger ant.

Juana had turned to look at him and she saw his back stiffen.

"How far?" she asked quietly.

"They will be here by evening," said Kino. He looked up the long steep chimney of the cleft where the water came down. "We must go east," he said, and his eyes searched the stone shoulder behind the cleft. And thirty feet up on the gray shoulder he saw a

John Steinbeck, who lived from 1902 to 1968, was an American writer of short stories and novels. He is known for his realistic view of poverty and its effect on people. Among his best-known works are *The Grapes of Wrath, Tortilla Flat,* and *Of Mice and Men.*

---

utterly: *Completely.*
weary: *Very tired. "Juana slumped to her knees" is a clue.*
petulant: *Showing a bad temper. ". . . he cried softly" is a clue.*
rigid: *Not bending or moving (*rigi- *refers to stiff).*

cleft: *A split or division between two parts.*

La Paz is a city in northwest Mexico. It is located on the Baja California peninsula between the Gulf of California and the Pacific Ocean (see map). The city itself is considered to be a pearl fishing center. However, most of the people here struggle daily to overcome poor economic conditions.

series of little erosion caves. He slipped off his sandals and clambered up to them, gripping the bare stone with his toes, and he looked into the shallow caves. They were only a few feet deep, wind-hollowed scoops, but they sloped slightly downward and back. Kino crawled into the largest one and lay down and knew that he could not be seen from the outside. Quickly he went back to Juana.

"You must go up there. Perhaps they will not find us there," he said.

Without questions she filled her water bottle to the top, and then Kino helped her up to the shallow cave and brought up the packages of food and passed them to her. And Juana sat in the cave entrance and watched him. She saw that he did not try to erase their tracks in the sand. Instead, he climbed up the brush cliff beside the water, clawing and tearing at the ferns and wild grape as he went. And when he had climbed a hundred feet to the next bench he came down again. He looked carefully at the smooth rock shoulder toward the cave to see that there was no trace of passage, and at last he climbed up and crept into the cave beside Juana.

"When they go up," he said, "we will slip away, down to the lowlands again. I am afraid only that the baby may cry. You must see that he does not cry."

"He will not cry," she said, and she raised the baby's face to her

---

erosion: The action or result of wearing away by nature.
clambered: Climbed with difficulty.
scoops: Here it means rounded cavities or holes.

clawing: Scratching or digging into a surface as if with claws.

own and looked into his eyes and he stared solemnly back at her.

"He knows," said Juana.

Now Kino lay in the cave entrance, his chin braced on his crossed arms, and he watched the blue shadow of the mountain move out across the brushy desert below until it reached the Gulf, and the long twilight of the shadow was over the land.

The trackers were long in coming, as though they had trouble with the trail Kino had left. It was dusk when they came at last to the little pool. And all three were on foot now, for a horse could not climb the last steep slope. From above they were thin figures in the evening. The two trackers scurried about on the little beach, and they saw Kino's progress up the cliff before they drank. The man with the rifle sat down and rested himself, and the trackers squatted near him, and in the evening the points of their cigarettes glowed and receded. And then Kino could see that they were eating, and the soft murmur of their voices came to him.

Then darkness fell, deep and black in the mountain cleft. The animals that used the pool came near and smelled men there and drifted away again into the darkness.

He heard a murmur behind him. Juana was whispering, "Coyotito." She was begging him to be quiet. Kino heard the baby whimper, and he knew from the muffled sounds that Juana had covered his head with her shawl.

Down on the beach a match flared, and in its momentary light Kino saw that two of the men were sleeping, curled up like dogs, while the third watched, and he saw the glint of the rifle in the match light. And then the match died, but it left a picture on Kino's eyes. He could see it, just how each man was, two sleeping curled and the third squatting in the sand with the rifle between his knees.

Kino moved silently back into the cave. Juana's eyes were two sparks reflecting a low star. Kino crawled quietly close to her and he put his lips near to her cheek.

"There is a way," he said.

"But they will kill you."

"If I get first to the one with the rifle," Kino said, "I must get to him first, then I will be all right. Two are sleeping."

Her hand crept out from under her shawl and gripped his arm. "They will see your white clothes in the starlight."

"No," he said. "And I must go before moonrise."

---

solemnly: Deeply serious.
braced: Supported or held upright.
twilight: The soft, dim light that fills the sky after sunset (twi- here means half).
scurried: Moved quickly, with light, short steps.
squatted: Sat on one's heels.
receded: Here it means seemed farther away.

murmur: The low sound of voices, slightly above a whisper.
whimper: Cry or sob softly.
muffled: Deadened by a covering. ". . . covered his head with her shawl" is a clue.
flared: Burned or shone brightly for a short time. ". . . in its momentary light" is a clue.
glint: A flash of light or sparkle.

He searched for a soft word and then gave it up. "If they kill me," he said, "lie quietly. And when they are gone away, go to Loreto."

Her hand shook a little, holding his wrist.

"There is no choice," he said. "It is the only way. They will find us in the morning."

Her voice trembled a little. "Go with God," she said.

He peered closely at her and he could see her large eyes. His hand fumbled out and found the baby, and for a moment his palm lay on Coyotito's head. And then Kino raised his hand and touched Juana's cheek, and she held her breath.

Against the sky in the cave entrance Juana could see that Kino was taking off his white clothes, for dirty and ragged though they were they would show up against the dark night. His own brown skin was a better protection for him. And then she saw how he hooked his amulet neck-string about the horn handle of his great knife, so that it hung down in front of him and left both hands free. He did not come back to her. For a moment his body was black in the cave entrance, crouched and silent, and then he was gone.

Juana moved to the entrance and looked out. She peered like an owl from the hole in the mountain, and the baby slept under the blanket on her back, his face turned sideways against her neck and shoulder. She could feel his warm breath against her skin, and Juana whispered her combination of prayer and magic, her Hail Marys[1] and her ancient intercession, against the black unhuman things.

The night seemed a little less dark when she looked, and to the east there was a lightning in the sky, down near the horizon where the moon would show. And, looking down, she could see the cigarette of the man on watch.

Kino edged like a slow lizard down the smooth rock shoulder. He had turned his neck-string so that the great knife hung down from his back and could not clash against the stone. His spread fingers gripped the mountain, and his bare toes found support through contact, and even his chest lay against the stone so that he would not slip. For any sound, a rolling pebble or a sigh, a little slip of flesh on rock, would rouse the watchers below. Any sound that was not germane to the night would make them alert. But the night was not silent; the little tree frogs that lived near the stream twittered like birds, and the high metallic ringing of the cicadas filled the mountain cleft. And Kino's own music was in his head, the music of the enemy, low and pulsing, nearly asleep. But the Song of the Family had become as fierce and sharp and feline as the snarl of a female puma. The family song was alive now and driving him down on the dark enemy. The harsh cicada seemed to take up its melody, and the twittering tree frogs called little phrases of it.

And Kino crept silently as a shadow down the smooth mountain face. One bare foot moved a few inches and the toes touched the stone and gripped, and the other foot a few inches, and then the palm of one hand a little downward, and then the other hand, until the whole body, without seeming to move, had moved. Kino's mouth was open so that even his breath would make no sound, for he knew that he was not invisible. If the watcher, sensing movement, looked at the dark place against the stone which was his body, he could see him. Kino must move so slowly he would not draw the watcher's eyes. It took him a long time to reach the bottom and to crouch behind a little dwarf palm. His heart

---

amulet: *A charm against evil.*
crouched: *Bent down with limbs close to the body.*
intercession: *A plea (in this case to God) on behalf of others (inter-means between; -ces- refers to going).*
rouse: *Bring to attention or awaken.*
germane: *Related to or consistent with.*

twittered: *Chirped lightly.*
metallic: *Like metal.*
cicadas: *Flying insects that make a dull humming sound.*
feline: *Like a cat. ". . . fierce and sharp . . . as the snarl of a female puma" is a clue.*
puma: *A mountain lion.*

thundered in his chest and his hands and face were wet with sweat. He crouched and took slow long breaths to calm himself.

Only twenty feet separated him from the enemy now, and he tried to remember the ground between. Was there any stone which might trip him in his rush? He kneaded his legs against cramp and found that his muscles were jerking after their long tension. And then he looked apprehensively to the east. The moon would rise in a few moments now, and he must attack before it rose. He could see the outline of the watcher, but the sleeping men were below his vision. It was the watcher Kino must find—must find quickly and without hesitation. Silently he drew the amulet string over his shoulder and loosened the loop from the horn handle of his great knife.

He was too late, for as he rose from his crouch the silver edge of the moon slipped above the eastern horizon, and Kino sank back behind his bush.

It was an old and ragged moon, but it threw hard light and hard shadow into the mountain cleft, and now Kino could see the seated figure of the watcher on the little beach beside the pool. The watcher gazed full at the moon, and then he lighted another cigarette, and the match illuminated his dark face for a moment. There could be no waiting now; when the watcher turned his head,

Kino must leap. His legs were as tight as wound springs.

And then from above came a little murmuring cry. The watcher turned his head to listen and then he stood up, and one of the sleepers stirred on the ground and awakened and asked quietly, "What is it?"

"I don't know," said the watcher. "It sounded like a cry, almost like a human—like a baby."

The man who had been sleeping said, "You can't tell. Some coyote bitch with a litter. I've heard a coyote pup cry like a baby."

The sweat rolled in drops down Kino's forehead and fell into his eyes and burned them. The little cry came again and the watcher looked up the side of the hill to the dark cave.

"Coyote maybe," he said, and Kino heard the harsh click as he cocked the rifle.

---

kneaded: (pronounced "nĕd-ĭd") *Here it means squeezed or massaged. "...his legs against cramp" is a clue.*
apprehensively: *Fearfully; uneasily.*
illuminated: *Lit up (il- means in; -lumin- means light).*

bitch: *A female dog or similar animal.*
litter: *The baby animals produced during one birth.*
cocked: *Put the hammer of a gun in position for firing. "Kino heard the harsh click" is a clue.*

"If it's a coyote, this will stop it," the watcher said as he raised the gun.

Kino was in mid-leap when the gun crashed and the barrel-flash made a picture on his eyes. The great knife swung and crunched hollowly. It bit through neck and deep into chest, and Kino was a terrible machine now. He grasped the rifle even as he wrenched free his knife. His strength and his movement and his speed were a machine. He whirled and struck the head of the seated man like a melon. The third man scrabbled away like a crab, slipped into the pool, and then he began to climb frantically, to climb up the cliff where the water penciled down. His hands and feet thrashed in the tangle of the wild grapevine, and he whimpered and gibbered as he tried to get up. But Kino had become as cold and deadly as steel. Deliberately he threw the lever of the rifle, and then he raised the gun and aimed deliberately and fired. He saw his enemy tumble backward into the pool, and Kino strode to the water. In the moonlight he could see the frantic frightened eyes, and Kino aimed and fired between the eyes.

And then Kino stood uncertainly. Something was wrong, some signal was trying to get through to his brain. Tree frogs and cicadas were silent now. And then Kino's brain cleared from its red concentration and he knew the sound— the keening, moaning, rising hysterical cry from the little cave in the side of the stone mountain, the cry of death.

Everyone in La Paz remembers the return of the family; there may be some old ones who saw it, but those whose fathers and whose grandfathers told it to them remember it nevertheless. It is an event that happened to everyone.

It was late in the golden afternoon when the first little boys ran hysterically in the town and spread the word that Kino and Juana were coming back. And everyone hurried to see them. The sun was settling toward the western mountains and the shadows on the ground were long. And perhaps that was what left the deep impression on those who saw them.

The two came from the rutted country road into the city, and they were not walking in single file, Kino ahead and Juana behind, as usual, but side by side. The sun was behind them and their long shadows stalked ahead, and they seemed to carry two towers of darkness with them. Kino had a rifle across his arm and Juana carried her shawl like a sack over her shoulder. And in it was a small limp heavy bundle. The shawl was crusted with dried blood, and the bundle swayed a little as she walked. Her face was hard and lined and leathery with fatigue and with the tightness with which she fought fatigue. And her wide eyes stared inward on herself. She was as remote and as removed as Heaven. Kino's lips were thin and his jaws tight, and the people say that he carried fear with him, that he was as dangerous as a rising storm. The people say that the two seemed to be removed from human experience; that they had gone through pain and had come out on the other side; that there was almost a magical protection about them. And those people who had rushed to see them crowded back and let them pass and did not speak to them.

Kino and Juana walked through the city as though it were not there. Their eyes glanced neither right nor left nor up nor down, but stared only straight ahead. Their legs moved a little jerkily, like well-made wooden dolls, and they carried pillars of black fear about them. And as they walked through the stone and plaster city

---

wrenched: Suddenly twisted.
scrabbled: Made quick, scraping movements.
thrashed: Moved about wildly.
gibbered: Spoke nonsense.
strode: Moved with long, confident steps (the past tense of *stride*).
keening: Loud wailing.

hysterical: Showing uncontrollable emotion.
rutted: Having deep tracks usually made by the wheels of vehicles.
stalked: Here it means walked or moved angrily.
remote: Far away (re- means back or away; -mote refers to moving).
"...and as removed as Heaven" is a clue.
pillars: Columns or vertical structures used for support.

down the shore toward the water. . . .

And when they came to the water's edge they stopped and stared out over the Gulf. And then Kino laid the rifle down, and he dug among his clothes, and then he held the great pearl in his hand. He looked into its surface and it was gray and ulcerous. Evil faces peered from it into his eyes, and he saw the light of burning. And in the surface of the pearl he saw the frantic eyes of the man in the pool. And in the surface of the pearl he saw Coyotito lying in the little cave with the top of his head shot away. And the pearl was ugly; it was gray, like a malignant growth. And Kino heard the music of the pearl, distorted and insane. Kino's hand shook a little, and he turned slowly to Juana and held the pearl out to her. She stood beside him, still holding her dead bundle over her shoulder. She looked at the pearl in his hand for a moment and then she looked into Kino's eyes and said softly, "No, you."

And Kino drew back his arm and flung the pearl with all his might. Kino and Juana watched it go, winking and glimmering under the setting sun. They saw the little splash in the distance, and they stood side by side watching the place for a long time.

And the pearl settled into the lovely green water and dropped toward the bottom. The waving branches of the algae called to it and beckoned to it. The lights on its surface were green and lovely. It settled down to the sand bottom among the fern-like plants. Above, the surface of the water was a green mirror. And the pearl lay on the floor of the sea. A crab scampering over the bottom raised a little cloud of sand, and when it settled the pearl was gone.

And the music of the pearl drifted to a whisper and disappeared.

brokers peered at them from barred windows and servants put one eye to a slitted gate and mothers turned the faces of their youngest children inward against their skirts. Kino and Juana strode side by side through the stone and plaster city and down among the brush houses, and the neighbors stood back and let them pass. . . .

In Kino's ears the Song of the Family was as fierce as a cry. He was immune and terrible, and his song had become a battle cry. They trudged past the burned square where their house had been without even looking at it. They cleared the brush that edged the beach and picked their way

---

slitted: *Made of narrow strips of material with spaces between them.*
immune: *Here it means not affected by or responsive to surroundings.*
trudged: *Walked as though one's feet were very heavy.*
picked their way: *Went slowly and carefully to avoid obstacles.*
ulcerous: *Like an open sore.*
peered: *Looked.*
malignant: *Very harmful (mal- means bad or evil).*

distorted: *Twisted (-tort- means to twist).*
flung: *Threw violently or with force (the past tense of* fling*).*
with all his might: *With all his strength.*
algae: *A group of sea plants, including seaweed.*
beckoned: *Invited someone or something to come using a nod or a gesture.*
fern-like: *Like a fern, a flowerless green plant.*
scampering: *Running hurriedly or playfully.*

Thinking about Your Prereading Reactions

Return to the questions on page 45. Think again about the message of the poem "Carmel Point" as it relates to the title "All That Glitters." Does Steinbeck's story about the pearl have a similar message? What is it?

Understanding Intended Meaning

Discuss the following questions with your class.

tdk tale.

1. While at the pool of water, Kino cannot rest as he wanted to. Why? Is he afraid? How do you know? What is he afraid of?

2. Where does Kino lead Juana and the baby? For what reason? What is his plan?

3. What is he afraid Coyotito will do? What is Juana's reaction to this fear?

4. Describe the actions of the trackers when they arrive at the pool.

5. What does Kino plan to do? Why must he get to the pool before moonrise? Why does he remove his clothes?

6. How does Kino feel about his wife and baby? How do you know?

7. Is Kino successful in carrying out his plans? Why or why not?

8. What happens to Coyotito?

9. Describe Kino and Juana's return to the village. Has their relationship to one another changed? If so, how do you know? How do the people of the village react to them? phan ưng .

10. What images does Kino see in the pearl at the end of the story? What does he do with the pearl?

Now read the story again before proceeding to the following activities. This time you may want to examine more carefully any details you did not fully understand during your first reading.

Relating to Self

Discuss one or both of the following questions with a small group.

1. If you were Kino, is there anything you might have done differently to avoid the tragedy that occurred?
2. Did Kino do the right thing by throwing the pearl back into the sea at the end? What would you have done with it had you been Kino?

Exploring the Conflict

Every story has a conflict that is the result of tension between two important story elements: a protagonist and an antagonist. The protagonist is a main character or group of characters who desire something (the main goal). The antagonist is usually another character or group of characters who, either directly or indirectly, work to prevent the protagonist from reaching the main goal. The antagonist does not necessarily have to be other characters, however. It can be nature or an idea (good or bad) that is within the protagonist. The conflict between the protagonist and the antagonist builds throughout the story, causing a great deal of tension. The high point of the tension is called the climax, and the ending is called the resolution.

The tension line looks something like this:

climax

protagonist

antagonist

resolution

Now look again at *The Pearl* and identify the following story elements:

the protagonist: _____

the protagonist's main goal: _____

the antagonist: _____

the climax: _____

the resolution: _____

Discuss your answer with your class and the teachers.

Appreciating Descriptive Language

1. Authors often draw their readers into the excitement of a story by appeals to the senses: sight, sound, smell, touch, and taste. For example, John Steinbeck makes the night come alive by appealing to the reader's sense of sound with the words "the little tree frogs that lived near the stream twittered like birds..." (page 49). Find several passages from the story that appeal to the senses listed below and place each in the appropriate category. There may be categories for which you can find no examples.

   Twittered : tiếng nói líu.

   sight: _____

   sound: _____

   smell: _____

   touch: _____

   taste: _____

   Discuss your examples with a small group. You may want to add other examples to your list based on what you learn from your classmates.

2. Descriptive language often involves a comparison between two things that are not usually thought to be similar in any way. For example, the statement *your bicycle leaped forward like a cat* uses such a comparison. Bicycles and cats are not usually compared to one another. Look at the comparisons from the story in the chart on page 56. Explain each one in the column provided. Then find one additional example of your own to place in the last space.

Comparison	Explanation
Example: ". . . Kino was a terrible machine" (page 51).	Kino is compared to a machine because he seemed to be fighting without any human feelings or pity for the trackers.
". . . two of the men were sleeping, curled up like dogs" (page 48).	
"And Kino crept silently as a shadow down the smooth mountain face" (page 49).	
"In Kito's ears the song of the family was as fierce as a cry".	

Discuss each comparison with your class and the teacher.

3. What does Steinbeck mean when he talks about the "music of the pearl," the "Song of the Family," and the "music of the enemy"? Why does he compare the movements of people's lives to music? Does this increase your enjoyment of the story? If so, how?

4. Steinbeck uses many words whose sounds suggest their meanings. The forming of such words is called *onomatopoeia* (pronounced "ŏn-ä-măt-ä-pē'-ä"). For example, Steinbeck uses onomatopoeia when he says that the baby "gurgled and clucked" against Juana's breast (see page 46). Find several other examples of onomatopoeia in the story.

Both the sea anemone and the pearl brought their victims something very unexpected. When events turn out to be the opposite of what we expect, we call it irony. The irony can be very dramatic, as in the following song by Paul Simon. The song describes Richard Cory, a man who had everything any man could ever want . . . or so it seemed.

The song "Richard Cory" is based on a poem by the same title that was written in the early part of the 1900s by Edwin Arlington Robinson, an American poet.

Richard Cory
Paul Simon

They say that Richard Cory
Owns one half of this whole town
With political connections
To spread his wealth around
Born into society,
A banker's only child
He had everything a man could want,
Power, grace, and style

Chorus:
But I work in his factory
And I curse the life I'm living
And I curse my poverty
And I wish that I could be
Oh, I wish that I could be
Oh, I wish that I could be
Richard Cory

The papers print his picture
Almost everywhere he goes
Richard Cory at the opera

Richard Cory at a show

And rumor of his parties

And the orgies on his yacht

Oh, he surely must be happy

With everything he's got

Chorus

He freely gave to charity

He had the common touch

They were grateful for his patronage

And they thanked him very much

So my mind was filled with wonder

When the evening headlines read

Richard Cory went home last night

And put a bullet through his head

Chorus

Discovering the Character

As you read the words of the song, you find that the character of Richard Cory is revealed. Discuss the following questions about Richard Cory with your class.

1. What personal characteristics of Richard Cory do you discover from the song? What lines support each?

Characteristic	**Supporting Lines**
Example: generous	*"He freely gave to charity . . . ."*

---

orgies: *Parties at which people give in to their immediate desires, showing little self-control.*

patronage: *Support, encouragement, or protection (a* patron *is someone who gives patronage; pat- refers to father).*

2. The song shocks us with the news of Richard Cory's suicide at the end. Why is this news so shocking? Why do you think he committed such an act? Is it possible that something important may have been missing in his life?

Relating to Self

Discuss one or both of the following questions with a partner.

1. Often in our own lives events turn out the opposite of what we expect. We say that these events are ironical. Have you experienced anything ironical in your own life? Have you noticed any irony in the life of anyone you know? Explain.

2. The factory worker in the song envied Richard Cory and wished that he could change places with him. Have you ever wished you could change places with someone and later realized that you were better off not being in the other person's place? Explain.

Developing Your Word Bank

Many of the more common words and phrases used in this unit reappear in other selections throughout the book. List in your Word Bank (see page 152) a few of the words or phrases that are new to you. Choose only those items that you feel will be useful. You may want to work with a partner or have your teacher help you with this task. Consider words you might want to use in conversation, in writing, or in communication about an academic area in which you have a special interest.

Ideas for Discussion and/or Writing

Choose one or more of the following activities.

1. Do you know of other songs, stories, or poems in which events turn out quite differently from what most readers expect? If so, share them with the members of your class. You may even want to help your class create a collection of such literature.

2. With a partner, write a different version of The Pearl. Begin at the point when Kino and Juana realize they are being followed by the trackers. Include in your story words and phrases that appeal to the senses (sight, sound, smell, touch, and taste). Share your story with other members of your class. You may want to act it out with the help of volunteers playing the various characters.

3. Write a letter to Kino telling him what you think he might have done to prevent the tragedy that occurred. Ask a partner to pretend to be Kino. Have your partner answer your letter, giving reasons that justify his actions in the story.

4. Choose a proverb (such as "All that glitters is not gold") from the culture you know best. Make sure you choose one that holds special meaning for you. Write about its importance to your own life and to the lives of those around you. Have a partner read what you have written and give you feedback. Ask your partner questions such as: Did I state my ideas clearly? What do you understand my ideas to be? Do you agree or disagree with them? What would you change in my paper if you were me?

5. If you found a great pearl such as the one Kino found, what would you do with the money it might bring? Discuss your specific plans. Are there any dangers of which you would beware? Consider what you have learned from Kino and Juana's experience. Compare your ideas with those of a partner.

6. Explore the conflict in one or more of the other stories that you have read so far in this book. In each case, identify the following elements: the protagonist, the protagonist's main goal, the antagonist, the climax, and the resolution. Compare your decisions with others who explored the same stories. Make any changes you want to make based on what you learn from your classmates.

Note

1. A Hail Mary is a prayer directed to Mary, the mother of Jesus, by Catholics.

5

THE POWER OF ILLUSION

Onstage Houdini had his hands and arms locked together with irons. Was he able to free himself?

We have all seen or heard about the unusual feats or achievements of people who were thought to have special powers. The feats may have involved unlikely escapes requiring great skill and courage. They may have involved lifting extremely heavy objects, showing tremendous strength. Or they may even have involved a type of sorcery (supernatural power). Share with a small group any stories you know about such feats and the people who were reported to have accomplished them.

from The Great Houdini

Lester David

The great Houdini was perhaps the best-known person in the Western world reported to have superhuman powers. He could escape with ease from iron-banded boxes and other such traps. He could make it appear that spirits from the dead were floating around a small, enclosed room. Were his feats magic? Or were they the result of something else? Read the following biographical sketch to find out.

A great blast from the tugboat McAllister signaled the noon hour as the muscular man leaped aboard. He announced he was ready and 5,000 persons lining the waterfront strained forward. Suddenly the voice of a woman rose above the hum of the crowd: "Stop him, somebody," she cried. "It's suicide!"

Aboard the tugboat Houdini, in black trunks and gray bathing shirt, called for the shackles. A man encircled his ankles with irons and clamped two sets of steel handcuffs around his wrists. Next, Houdini was helped into a packing case five feet long and a yard wide and deep. Heavy weights were attached outside. Then the case was swiftly nailed shut and reinforced with steel bands. Finally, it was tied with inch-thick rope.

A winch lowered the crate into the water, and a gasp, as though from a single throat, passed through the crowd as the box sank like a weight.

Seconds ticked away. The throng was hushed, their eyes fixed to the spot where the crate had disappeared.

More seconds passed. One man spoke for many in a whisper: "He can't. . . . he's finished." Fear tightened many faces.

Still silence from below.

Then, explosive as a porpoise leaping from the sea, a head broke the surface of the water. Harry Houdini, free of cuffs and irons, took a great gulp of air and was hauled aboard the tugboat. A roar burst from the crowd.

It had taken him exactly 52 seconds to escape.

This was only one of many feats performed during his lifetime by Harry Houdini, stage magician, and beyond question the greatest escape artist who ever lived.

The Superman of his age, the Great Houdini could free himself—often in a matter of seconds—from chains, barred cells, sealed chambers, underwater

blast: *Here it means the loud blowing of a horn.*
signaled: *Communicated or indicated without words.*
suicide: *The act of killing oneself (sui- refers to self; -cide means killing).*
trunks: *Men's shorts used for swimming.*

shackles: *Metal rings placed around the wrists or ankles to hinder movement. ". . . encircled his ankles" is a clue.*
winch: *A machine used to move heavy objects or cargo. ". . . lowered the crate" is a clue.*
porpoise: *A small whale with a rounded snout.*

containers, most handcuffs, iron boots, straitjackets—practically any type of restraint men could dream up. He escaped from drowning more than 2,000 times, freed himself from about 15,000 straitjackets, and picked some 12,000 locks.

During a career that covered more than forty years from the late 19th century to 1926, Houdini demonstrated to audiences all over the world that nothing could hold him. He earned a fortune performing on vaudeville stages and at circuses, world's fairs, and carnivals. He included kings, princes, and presidents among his friends and admirers; invited to give special shows before them, he never failed to mystify.

When the occasion moved him, which was often, Houdini would give public demonstrations of his powers in icy rivers, on the streets, in town squares, even in prisons!

Wherever he went, people used great ingenuity to devise something that could hold Houdini but none ever succeeded. On one of his world tours, for example, Russian secret police in Moscow dared him to escape from the *carette,* a movable cell used to transport political prisoners. The carette was nothing less than a safe on wheels, with thick steel walls and floor and two six-inch square vents. Houdini was searched by doctors, stripped to his shorts, and locked inside. In 45 minutes, he was out.

The man who was to gain worldwide fame as Houdini was born Ehrich Weiss in Budapest, Hungary, in 1874, the son of a poor rabbi. While he was still an infant, the family emigrated to Appleton, Wisconsin, where young Weiss spent his boyhood.

Locks, acrobatics, and magic held a fascination for him throughout his youth. He would hunt for locks in junkyards and take them home to study, to master. He would practice acrobatics by the hour. And he would learn how to perform the tricks of sideshow magicians and devise many of his own. These three accomplishments formed the basis of his fabulous career.

When he was sixteen, Ehrich's family moved to New York City, where he came across the memoirs of Robert-Houdin, the famous French magician and scientist known as the father of modern conjuring. Robert-Houdin became his guide and hero.

Ehrich Weiss soon changed his own name to Harry Houdini. At the age of nineteen, he teamed with his brother Theodore to perform a magic act at beach resorts. Within two years, the act broke up when Houdini married Beatrice Rahner, who became his new partner onstage as well.

They played freak shows, dime museums, small vaudeville houses, all sorts of cheap amusement places. Often they would have to give as many as a dozen

---

straitjackets: *Jackets that bind arms tightly to the sides of the body.*
restraint: *Something that limits or prevents movement.*
picked: *Here it means opened with a pick (a sharp tool).*
vaudeville: *A type of show consisting of a series of short acts performed for the entertainment of others.*
mystify: *Greatly puzzle (mysti- refers to secrecy).*
ingenuity: *Cleverness.*

rabbi: *An official religious leader of the Jewish faith.*
acrobatics: *Performance demonstrating skill in moving the body in various positions. Often balance is involved.*
sideshow: *A show performed in addition to the main show.*
memoirs: *A collection of personal experiences written down so that they may not be forgotten (mem- refers to remembering).*
conjuring: *Using magic to cause something to appear.*

shows each day for a grand total of $25 a week.

The acts consisted of routine "magic" tricks, an escape from a locked trunk, and a handcuff stunt. But audiences were convinced that the trunk would be snapped open from the inside and that the cuffs were specially made to be opened easily.

Soon Houdini decided to abandon magic and spend all his offstage hours inventing more difficult escapes.

He devised shackles, massive bolts, quadruple locks—adding showmanship and color to his wonders of escape. And when the feats were perfected, he unveiled them before audiences.

Houdini's fame really zoomed after he boldly challenged police in cities here and abroad to keep him locked up. In San Francisco, he freed himself from ten pairs of handcuffs, all clamped on his wrists at the same time. In London, he had no trouble ridding himself of the most advanced cuffs devised by experts.

What was the secret of Houdini's escapes?

HARRY HOUDINI THE JAIL BREAKER

INTRODUCING HIS <u>LATEST</u> & <u>GREATEST</u>

PRISON CELL & BARREL MYSTERY

HOUDINI is strapped & locked in a barrel placed in a police cell which is also locked and in less than 2 seconds changes places. **£100.** WILL BE PAID TO ANYONE FINDING TRAPS, PANELS OR FALSE DOORS IN THE CELL

After being strapped inside a barrel and locked inside a prison cell, Houdini released himself. An assistant was then found in the barrel where Houdini had been.

The master himself was the first to admit that "magic" had nothing to do with them. His feats were accomplished by a combination of many things. Trickery played a part, as it does with all stage magicians, but so did scientific know-how, an expert knowledge of locks, intense concentration, great physical strength and endurance, and a contortionist's body which enabled him to throw his limbs out of joint.

Let us discuss these in detail.

First, the tricks. Houdini himself revealed many of these during his lifetime. Others, of course, remain a mystery to this day.

Many handcuffs, he said, could be opened by striking the keyhole part sharply against a hard surface, such as a shoe or the floor. Sometimes he had a lead plate sewn into his trousers above the knee. He opened other handcuffs with a key he had hidden either on his person or somewhere in the closed cabinet he entered onstage.

Some of his steel collars had false hinges that

---

quadruple: *Having four parts* (quad- *means four*).
unveiled: *Here it means demonstrated openly to be viewed by all.*
contortionist: *A person who can twist his or her body and limbs into*

unusual positions (con- *means together;* -tort- *refers to twisting*).
" . . . *which enabled him to throw his limbs out of joint" is a clue.*

were undetectable even on closest examination. Houdini's famous "milk-can escape" always drew gasps. He would immerse himself in a large iron can filled with water, the top locked securely after him. Then a curtain would hide him from the audience. The secret lay in a false collar directly beneath the padlocked top. Houdini held his breath a while, then heaved upward. Off came the collar, locked top and all!

In the packing case feat described at the start of this essay, Houdini freed himself of his shackles while the box was being locked and iron-banded. He escaped from the case through a trick panel on the side, which was lightly nailed. When Houdini pressed a hidden spring, it turned inward. He replaced the panel before rising to the surface.

But tricks alone could never explain Houdini's exploits. He was one of the world's foremost experts on locks. He could solve the secret of the most complex ones after a moment's examination and would open them with tiny tools he had hidden on his person. His collection of lock picks might be hidden in a shoe, pasted to the sole of his foot, folded into a tiny penknife.

And for some escapes he needed no tools at all. Wrote Harold Kellock, in his biography of Houdini: "He could open the strongest steel vault as easily as a skilled second-story burglar could pry loose a bedroom window."

Houdini's powerful body, which he kept in perfect condition through training, was a key factor in many of his stunts. Certainly it took nearly superhuman strength to accomplish the "wet sheet escape." His hands bound to his sides with a cloth, he was rolled tightly inside three large sheets, one after the other. His ankles, knees, waist, and neck were bound in heavy

bandages and securely tied. Finally, the cloths were soaked in hot water to make them stick to his body. He would wriggle and struggle and sweat—but he would get out. "This test," he said, "is so hard that several times I have had barely enough strength to walk off the stage after it was over."

This was no trick. For early in life, he discovered he could twist his body into positions the average person could not. This ability helped him slip out of the tightest bonds. He once said: "To any young man who has in mind a career similar to mine, I would say: 'First try bending over backward and picking up a pin with your teeth from the floor, and work up from that into the more difficult exercises.' That was my first stunt."

One day, at a swimming pool in a New York hotel, Houdini was sealed into an air-tight iron cabinet. It was then lowered into the water. Every five minutes, he would ring a signal bell connected to a wire inside the cabinet to let everyone know he was all right. After one hour, thirty-one minutes, he signaled his wish to emerge . . . and he did, alive and well.

Doctors at the time believed there was only enough oxygen in the cabinet to support life for five minutes. Houdini proved that, by taking shallow breaths, he could conserve the small air supply to keep alive far longer. With his experiment, the great escape artist hoped to set an example for miners and others who might be buried, showing how they could prolong their lives long enough for aid to reach them.

There was another aspect of Houdini's career that commanded international attention: his never-ending battle to expose fraudulent spiritualists. Houdini was convinced that these professional spirit mediums were outright fakes

---

immerse: *Completely cover with or submerge in a liquid.*
heaved: *Here it means pushed or moved up with great effort.*
exploits: *Heroic acts.*
conserve: *Save or keep from being lost (-serv- refers to keeping or preserving). ". . . by taking shallow breaths" is a clue.*
expose: *Here it means reveal or unmask.*

fraudulent: *Dishonest or extremely misleading (fraud means trickery).*
spiritualists: *Here it means people who claim that the dead can communicate with the living. The rest of the paragraph offers many clues.*
mediums: *Here it means individuals who claim to have the power to communicate with the dead. See the sentences following for clues.*

who used a variety of tricks. To prove his point, Houdini himself conducted "seances" for friends, reproducing the spiritualists' effects so well that his guests were convinced he *did* possess special powers. How else, they said, could a luminous figure flit around the room like a flying spirit? Why, the "ghost" even touched the guests with his cold hands!

Houdini willingly exposed his own trick. He had hired a pair of acrobats and dressed one entirely in black so that he was invisible in the darkened room. The other, daubed with luminous paint, did a handstand on his partner's shoulders, so that he appeared to be floating around the room. Of course, it was he who touched the guests, with fingers dipped in icy water.

One by one, Houdini bared the fakers' tricks.

One fake amazed clients by seeming to know all their old addresses for years back. Explanation: He would dash out the back door to the public library down the block, where he looked at the old street directories on file.

One thing is sure though. Were he here today, Houdini would continue to challenge the many fortune tellers, mystics, and fast-dollar operators who are cheating innocent believers.

In October, 1926, Houdini, at the height of his career, lectured on spiritualism before students at McGill University in Montreal. An art student drew a picture of him as he spoke. The quick drawing delighted Houdini, who invited the youth to the theater where he was appearing.

On a Friday morning, the young man appeared with two friends. When the discussion touched on the importance of physical endurance in Houdini's feats, one youth asked if the magician could absorb powerful punches. Houdini, turning to pick up a letter, replied absently that he could if he had time to tighten his muscles. Interpreting this as an invitation, the young man punched Houdini hard in the side, several times.

The blows hurt but Houdini rubbed the area and forgot about it. That evening, the pain in his abdomen worsened. The next day, still in pain, he boarded a train for Detroit; but when he arrived, he was in agony and his temperature had reached 102°.[1] Nevertheless, he went on with his show.

At the end, however, near collapse, he was taken to a hospital where doctors found that the blows had ruptured his appendix and blood

---

seances: *Meetings at which people are said to receive messages from the dead through a medium.*
luminous: *Giving off light (* lumin- *means light).*

daubed: *Applied with quick strokes. ". . . with luminous paint" is a clue.*
ruptured: *Broken open (* rupt- *means to break).*

poisoning had set in. Given less than a day to live, Houdini's will and strength kept him alive an entire week.

On October 31, 1926, at the age of fifty-two, his great heart failed. Even then he gave the world one final shudder. For the great Houdini, who mystified the world with his own brand of sorcery, died on Halloween.

Halloween, the eve of "All-Saints Day," is on October 31. On this day, children in the United States dress in costumes and sometimes go door-to-door asking for treats or playing pranks. Some adults, too, get in on the action by dressing in costumes and attending parties. Are any special days similar to Halloween celebrated in the culture you know best?

Thinking about Your Prereading Reactions

Return to the paragraph on page 62. Think again about the people you discussed who were reported to have special powers. Do you think their feats were the result of magic, trickery, or something else? Does what you learned from the biographical sketch about Houdini help to logically explain some of the feats?

Understanding Intended Meaning

Discuss the following questions with your class.

1. Describe some of the devices that were used to restrain Houdini. How was he able to escape from each one? How much of his success was due to tricks? What other factors were involved?

2. What advice did Houdini give to those who might want a career similar to his? What do you think about this advice?

3. Tell about Houdini's boyhood. How did it lead him to his unusual career?

4. Describe Houdini's rise to fame.

5. How did Houdini expose the tricks of the spiritualists?

6. Consider the date on which Houdini died. Do you see anything unusual about this fact? Why might it give the world "one final shudder," as the author claims?

Now read the selection again before proceeding to the following activities. This time you may want to examine more carefully any details you did not fully understand during your first reading.

shudder: A trembling as if from great fear.

Determining the Main Idea

As you learned in Unit 2, the main idea of a story is the most important idea that the author is trying to express. Which of the following statements comes closest to expressing the main idea of "The Great Houdini"?

- ◆ Beware of fraudulent spiritualists.
- ✗ ◆ In his amazing career, Houdini proved himself to be a man of great strength, cleverness, and courage.
- ◆ Even persons born in poverty can rise to fame and fortune through persistence.
- ◆ Don't always believe what you see.
- ◆ Restraints used by police are not always effective in confining a person.

Discuss your answer with your class and the teacher.

Discovering the Character

Many adjectives could be used to describe Houdini. A few are listed below. Find one or two facts from the reading that indicate that Houdini had each of the following personal characteristics. Write the facts in the spaces provided.

boastful

Example: He boldly challenged police in many cities to lock him up.

_____

courageous

_____

_____

intelligent

_____

_____

agile and physically powerful

_____

_____

Did Houdini have additional characteristics (positive or negative) that you believe to be worthy of mention? Find the facts that support each one. After considering several of Houdini's characteristics, decide which you admire most. Which do you admire least? Discuss your ideas with your classmates.

Relating to Self

Discuss one or more of the following questions with a partner.

1. A hero is someone whom people respect because he or she shows unusual courage or in some other way seems to be above others. Houdini was considered a hero. Do you have a hero? Have you ever had a hero? How important is it to have one? Does there seem to be a shortage of heroes today? If so, why?

2. Have you ever been fooled by a fortune teller, mystic, or "fast-dollar" operator? If so, describe the experience. In what way(s) were you taken advantage of? How did you feel once you realized what had happened?

3. Which of Houdini's feats impressed you the most? Why did it make such an impression on you?

Appreciating Descriptive Language

Authors sometimes use exaggeration for effect in their writings. The term for such descriptive language is *hyperbole* (pronounced "hī-pûr-bä⁴-lē"). For example, the author of the biographical sketch about Houdini used hyperbole in the words

The Superman of his age, the Great Houdini could free himself—often in a matter of seconds . . . (page 63).

Discuss with your class and the teacher in what way this quote is an example of hyperbole. Find other lines from the selection in which such exaggerations occur. Write them below and explain how they are examples of hyperbole. *aw thai phang, lam quá mức*

Examples of hyperbole:

_____

_____

Does the use of hyperbole increase or decrease your enjoyment of this biographical sketch? Discuss your ideas with your class and the teacher.

Although many admire a person who demonstrates great feats, not all have the desire to develop such skills themselves. Shel Silverstein shares his own attitude in the following poem.

The Sword-Swallower

Shel Silverstein

The great sword-swallower Salomar,
  He wears no ties or collars.
   He leans back, opens up his mouth,
    And "Gulp," his sword he swallers.

   I guess he finds it fun to feel
    That steel down in his belly.
     It's fine for he, but as for me—
      I'll take some bread and jelly.

Understanding Intended Meaning

Read the poem again, this time with a partner. On the following lines, write what you and your partner think it means. How does the author feel about performing dangerous or amazing feats?

_____

_____

_____

Drawing Comparisons

How do you think Shel Silverstein's feelings about performing amazing or dangerous feats differ from Houdini's feelings? Do you think your own feelings about this subject come closer to those of Houdini or those of Silverstein? Discuss your ideas with a partner.

Taking Liberty with Language

Sometimes in literature authors use unusual forms of language. The term for this practice among authors is *literary license*. For example, in line four of the poem "swallers" is used instead of "swallows." In line seven "It's fine for he" is used instead of the standard "It's fine for him." Why do you think Shel Silverstein uses such forms? Does his use of literary license help or hinder your enjoyment of the poem? Discuss your answers with your class and the teacher.

Developing Your Word Bank

Many of the more common words and phrases used in this unit reappear in other selections throughout the book. List in your Word Bank (see page 152) a few of the words or phrases that are new to you. Choose only those items that you feel will be useful. You may want to work with a partner or have your teacher help you with this task. Consider words you might want to use in conversation, in writing, or in communication about an academic area in which you have a special interest.

Ideas for Discussion and/or Writing

Choose one or more of the following activities.

1. With a small group, write a story about a miraculous escape. In your story, you may develop your own superhuman personality or use Houdini as the subject. Have one student write down the story as the members of your group dictate it. Ask a volunteer from your group to read the story aloud to the whole class.

2. Do we as human beings ever shackle ourselves *mentally* rather than physically? If so, in what ways? To what extent are we able to escape? Develop this idea with two or three examples. Share your examples with a partner. You may want to write about them.

3. Find out as much as you can from others or from library sources about how Halloween is celebrated in the United States. Your teacher or the librarian may be able to help you in your search. Is Halloween all fun and merriment? What are its dangers? Many people have talked about eliminating the celebration of Halloween because of its dangers, especially for children. How do you feel about this? Is the celebration worth saving? Share your ideas with your class.

4. Because people of all generations are fascinated by Houdini's feats, several biographies have been written about him over the years. Select one from your library that appeals to you. You may want to consider the titles below. Note that the first one was referred to in the reading selection.

    Houdini: His Life-Story by Harold Kellock

    Houdini: The Man Who Walked through Walls by William Lindsay Gresham

    Houdini: A Pictorial Life by Milbourne Christopher

    What additional information did you gather about Houdini's life from the book you chose to read? Share what you learned with members of your class.

Note

1. The temperature 102° (102 degrees) is based on the Fahrenheit thermometer scale in which the freezing point is 32 degrees.

6

BETWEEN TWO CULTURES

Second Nature

Diana Chang

How do I feel
Fine wrist to small feet?
I cough Chinese.

The old China muses through me.
I am foreign to the new.
I sleep upon dead years.

Sometimes I dream in Chinese.
I dream my father's dreams.
I wake,
I wake, grown up
And someone else.

I am the thin edge I sit on.
I begin to gray—white and in between.
My hair is America.

New England[1] moonlights in me.

I attend what is Chinese
In everyone.

We are in the air.

I shuttle passportless within myself,
My eyes slant around both hemispheres,
Gaze through walls

And long still be
Accustomed,
At home here,

Strange to say.

---

muses: *Here it means brings about a state of thought.*
moonlights: *A poetic way to say enchants.*
shuttle: *Travel back and forth. "... passportless within myself"*
is a clue.

hemispheres: *Here it means the eastern and western halves of the*
world (hemi- means half; -sphere- means ball or globe).

Are you now between two cultures?
If not, think about what it might be like
to be between two cultures. What
advantages and disadvantages do you
think there might be? In what ways are
your feelings similar to those expressed
in the poem on the previous page? If you
are now between two cultures, are others
from your first culture going through
this experience with you? If so, what
effect are they having on your
adjustment? Discuss with a small group.

Predicting Events

Read only to the bottom of page 78. With your classmates, make predictions about
what you think will happen and how the story will end. Have a volunteer record the
predictions where everyone can see them. Then finish reading the story and find out
which predictions came closest to what actually happened.

In his story below, Amado Muro describes with humor and some sadness what it is like to be between two cultures in the United States during the 1960s. Are his experiences very different from what newcomers experience today? To complicate the situation, Amado innocently falls in love with an "older woman" others call La Americana.

from Cecilia Rosas
Amado Muro

When I was in the ninth grade at Bowie High School in El Paso, I got a job hanging up women's coats at La Feria Department Store on Saturdays. It wasn't the kind of job that had much appeal for a Mexican boy or for boys of any other nationality, either. But the work wasn't hard, only boring. Wearing a smock, I stood around the Ladies' Wear Department all day long waiting for women customers to finish trying on coats so I could hang them up.

Having to wear a smock was worse than the work itself. But working in Ladies' Wear had two compensations: earning three dollars every Saturday was one; being close to Cecilia Rosas was the other.

Since I was only fourteen and in love for the first time, I looked at her more chastely than most. Her rich olive skin was almost as dark as mine. Sometimes she wore a rose in her hair. When she did, she looked so very lovely I forgot all about what La Feria was paying me to do and stood gaping at her instead.

She prided herself on being more American than Mexican because she was born in El Paso. And she did her best to act, dress, and talk the way Americans do. She hated to speak Spanish, disliked her Mexican name. She called herself Cecile Roses instead of Cecilia Rosas. This made the other salesladies smile derisively. They called her La Americana every time they mentioned her name.

Miss Rosas could be frivolous or serious, molding herself to each customer's personality. Her voice was the richest, the softest, I had ever heard. Hearing it made me want to dream, and I did. Romantic thoughts burgeoned up in my mind like rosy billows of hope scented with Miss Rosas's perfume. These thoughts made me so languid at my work that the floor manager, Joe Apple, warned me to show some enthusiasm for it or else suffer the consequences.

I had neither the desire nor the energy to respond to Joe Apple's warnings. Looking at Miss Rosas used up so much of my energy that I had little left for my work. Miss Rosas was twenty, much too old for me, everyone said. But what everyone said didn't matter. While I watched, I dreamed of being a hero. It hurt me to have her see me doing such menial work. But there was no escape from it. I needed the job to stay in school. So more and more I took refuge in dreams.

---

smock: *A loose, lightweight coatlike covering worn to protect one's clothes while working.*
compensations: *Things received which are equal to or which make up for things lost.*
chastely: *Purely or innocently. "Since I was only fourteen and in love for the first time" is a clue.*
gaping: *Staring in wonder with one's mouth open.*
prided: *Took pride in.*
derisively: *In a manner that makes fun of someone or something.*

"They called her La Americana" is a clue.
frivolous: *Silly or lighthearted.*
burgeoned: *Grew rapidly. "... like rosy billows of hope" is a clue.*
languid: *Without energy; slow (langu- refers to being faint or weak). The fact that he was warned to "show some enthusiasm" is a clue.*
consequences: *The results that naturally follow an action or condition (con- means with; -seque- means to follow). "... or else suffer" is a clue.*
menial: *Typical of a servant. "It hurt me" is a clue.*
refuge: *Here it means an escape.*

When I had watched her as much, if not more, than I could safely do without attracting the attention of other alert salesladies, I slipped out of Ladies' Wear and walked up the stairs to the top floor. There I sat on a window ledge, looking down at the city's canyons, and best of all, thinking about Miss Rosas and myself.

The dreams I dreamed were imaginative masterpieces, or so I thought. They transformed me from a colorless Mexican boy who put women's coats away into the American, handsome, dashing, and worldly, that I longed to be for her sake.

But my window-ledge reveries left me bewildered and shaken. The more thrillingly romantic fantasies I created, the more I needed to create.

So I spent less time in Ladies' Wear. My flights to the window ledge became more recklessly frequent. Sometimes I got tired sitting there. When I did, I took the freight elevator down to the street floor and brazenly walked out of the store without so much as punching a time clock. Walking the streets quickened my imagination, gave form and color to my thoughts. So absorbed was I in thoughts of Miss Rosas and myself that I bumped into Americans, apologizing mechanically in Spanish instead of English.

I thought about every word Miss Rosas had ever said to me, making myself believe she looked at me with unmistakable tenderness when she said them. When she said, "Amado, please hang up this fur coat," I found special meaning in her tone. It was as though she had said, "Amadito,[2] I love you."

When she gave these orders, I rushed into action like a man blazing with a desire to perform epically heroic feats. At such times I felt

capable of putting away not one but a thousand fur coats, and would have done so joyously.

Sometimes on the street I caught myself murmuring, "Cecilia, I love you." And so I emptied my heart on the streets and window ledge while women's coats piled up in Ladies' Wear.

But my absences didn't go unnoticed. Gruff warnings and stern admonitions came from executives. All the threats in the world couldn't have made me give up my window-ledge reveries or kept me from roaming city streets with Cecilia Rosas's name on my lips like a prayer.

The reports merely made me more cunning, more determined. I timed my absences more precisely and contrived better lies to explain them. Sometimes I went to the men's room and looked at myself in the mirror for as long as ten minutes at a time. Such self-studies filled me with gloom. Only my hair gave me hope. It was thick and wavy, deserving a better face to go with it. So I did the best I could with what I had, and combed it over my temples in ringlets just like the poets back in my hometown used to do.

Then one day something happened that almost made my overstrained heart stop beating. . . .

dashing: *Dressed in the latest fashions. This word is seldom used today.*
reveries: *Daydreams. The next sentence is a clue.*
brazenly: *Boldly. ". . . without so much as punching a time clock" is a clue.*
punching a time clock: *Placing a card in a machine that records the exact time. A time clock is used to record how many hours a person has worked.*
epically heroic feats: *Great deeds that are similar to what heroes might accomplish in epics (long poems that tell stories). The following*

sentence is a clue.
gruff: *Harsh.*
admonitions: *Warnings or advice. "Gruff warnings" is a clue.*
executives: *Persons running a company or organization.*
cunning: *Sly.*
precisely: *Exactly. "I timed my absences" is a clue.*
contrived: *Invented. ". . . better lies" is a clue.*

It happened on the day Miss Rosas stood behind me while I put a fur coat away. Her heady perfume, the fragrance of her warm healthy body, made me feel faint. I smiled and asked her in Spanish how she was feeling.

"Amado, speak English," she told me. "And pronounce the words slowly and carefully, so you don't sound like a country Mexican."

Then she looked at me in a way that made me the happiest employee who ever punched La Feria's time clock.

"Amadito," she whispered the way I had always dreamed she would.

"Yes, Cecilia," I said expectantly.

Her smile was warmly intimate. "Amadito, when are you going to take me to the movies?" she asked.

Other salesladies watched us, all smiling. They made me so nervous I couldn't answer.

"Amadito, you haven't answered me," Miss Rosas said teasingly. "Either you're bashful as a village sweetheart, or else you don't like me at all."

In voluble Spanish, I quickly assured her the latter wasn't the case. I was just getting ready to say, "Cecilia, I more than like you; I love you" when she frowned and told me to speak English. So I slowed down and tried to smooth out my ruffled thoughts.

"Cecilia," I said, "I'd love to take you to the movies any time."

Miss Rosas smiled and patted my cheek. "Will you buy me candy and popcorn?" she said.

I nodded, putting my hand against the imprint her warm palm had left on my face.

"And hold my hand?"

I said "yes" so enthusiastically it made her laugh. Other salesladies laughed too. Dazed and numb with happiness, I watched Miss Rosas walk away. How proud and confident she was. Other salesladies were looking at me and laughing.

This embarrassed me, but it wasn't altogether unpleasant. Miss Sandoval winked at Miss de la Rosa, then looked back at me.

"Don't go too fast with the Americana, Amado," she said. "Remember the procession is long and the candles are small."

They laughed and slapped me on the back. They all wanted to know when I was going to take Miss Rosas to the movies. "She didn't say," I blurted out without thinking.

This brought another burst of laughter. It drove me back up to the window ledge, where I thought about the wonderful thing that had happened. But I was too nervous to stay there. So I went to the men's room and looked at myself in the mirror again, wondering why Miss Rosas liked me so well. The mirror made it brutally clear that my looks hadn't influenced her. So it must have been something else, perhaps character. But that didn't seem likely either. Joe Apple had told me I didn't have much of that. Anyway, it was time for another walk. So I took one.

This time I trudged through Little Chihuahua, where both Miss Rosas and I lived. Little Chihuahua looked different to me that day. On that clear frosty day it was the world's most romantic place because Cecilia Rosas lived there.

---

heady: *Here it means capable of overwhelming the senses.*
intimate: *Familiar or close.*
voluble: *Fluent.*
latter: *The second of two items mentioned.*
ruffled: *Disturbed.*
dazed: *Stunned or overwhelmed. ". . . numb with happiness" is a clue.*

procession: *A group of people or things moving forward in a line (pro- means forward; -ces- refers to going). Here it refers to a wedding procession through life.*
blurted out: *Said quickly without thought.*
brutally: *Painfully (a brute is an animal without feeling).*
trudged: *Walked slowly with heavy feet.*

While walking, I reasoned that Miss Rosas might want to go dancing after the movies. So I went to Professor Toribio Ortega's dance studio and made arrangements to take my first lesson. Some neighborhood boys saw me when I came out. It didn't matter. On my lunch hour I went back and took my first lesson anyway. Professor Ortega danced with me. Softened by weeks of dreaming, I went limp in his arms imagining he was Miss Rosas.

The rest of the day was the same as many others before it. As usual I spent most of it stealing glances at Miss Rosas and slipping up to the window ledge. She looked busy, not like a woman in love.

When the day's work was done, I plodded home from the store just as dreamily as I had gone to it. And I told my sister all about what had happened to me. She looked at me thoughtfully, then combed my hair back with her fingertips as though trying to soothe me. "Amado," she said softly. "I wouldn't . . . " Then she looked away and shrugged her shoulders.

On Monday I borrowed three dollars from my Uncle Rodolfo without telling him what it was for. Miss Rosas hadn't told me what night she wanted me to take her to the movies. But the way she had looked at me made me think that almost any night would do. So I decided on Friday. Waiting for it to come was hard, but I had to keep my mind occupied. So I went to Zamora's newsstand to get the Alma Nortena songbook. Poring through it for the most romantic song I could find, I decided on "La Cecilia."

All week long I practiced singing it on my way to school and in the shower after basketball practice. But except for singing this song, I tried not to speak Spanish at all. At home I made my mother mad by saying in English, "Please pass the sugar."

I went on speaking English even though my mother and uncle didn't understand it. This shocked my sisters as well. When they asked me to explain my behavior, I parroted Miss Rosas, saying, "We're living in the United States now."

My rebellion against being a Mexican created an uproar. But it wasn't only the Spanish language that I lashed out against. I complained, "Can't we ever eat roast beef or ham and eggs like Americans do?"

My mother didn't speak to me for two days after that. My Uncle Rodolfo grimaced and mumbled something about renegade Mexicans who want to eat ham and eggs.

Life at home was almost intolerable. Cruel jokes and mocking laughter made it so. My sister Consuelo suggested I go to the courthouse and change my name to Beloved Wall, which is English for Amado Muro. My mother didn't agree. With a family like mine, how could I ever hope to become an American and win Miss Rosas?

Friday came at last. I put on my only suit, slicked my hair down with liquid vaseline, and doused myself with perfume.

"Amado's going to serenade that pretty girl everyone calls La Americana," my sister Consuelo told my mother and uncle when I sat down to eat. "Then he's going to take her to the movies."

This made my uncle laugh and my mother scowl.

"What nerve that boy's got," my uncle said, "to serenade a twenty-year-old woman."

---

plodded: *Moved with heavy steps.*
poring through: *Here it means reading carefully.*
lashed out: *Attacked or threatened, here verbally.*
grimaced: *Showed disgust by twisting the face out of shape.*
renegade: *A person who has rejected one group or tradition in favor of another (here -neg- means to deny). " . . . who want to eat ham and eggs" is a clue.*

intolerable: *Unbearable (in- here means not; -toler- means to bear). Related to* tolerate *which means to bear or put up with. "Cruel jokes and mocking laughter" is a clue.*
slicked: *Smoothed down, usually with an oily substance.*
vaseline: *An oily, greasy substance.*
doused: *Wet thoroughly. " . . . with perfume" is a clue.*
serenade: *Perform music for someone, usually one's lover.*

They made me so nervous I forgot to take off my cap when I sat down to eat.

"Amado, take off your cap," my mother said.

My uncle frowned. "All this boy thinks about is kissing girls," he said gruffly.

"But my boy's never kissed one," my mother said proudly.

My sister Consuelo laughed. "That's because they won't let him," she said.

This wasn't true. But I couldn't say so in front of my mother. I had already kissed Emalina Uribe from Porfirio Diaz Street not once but twice. Both times I'd kissed her in a darkened doorway less than a block from her home. But the kisses were over so soon we hardly had time to enjoy them. This was because Ema was afraid her big brother, the husky one nicknamed Toro, would see us. But if we'd had more time, it would have been better, I knew.

Along about six o'clock the three musicians who called themselves the Mariachis of Tecalitlan came by and whistled for me, just as they had said they would.

My mother shook her head when she saw them. "Son, who ever heard of serenading a girl at six o'clock in the evening," she said. "When your father had the mariachis sing for me, it was always at two o'clock in the morning—the only proper time."

But I got out my guitar anyway. I put on my cap and rushed out to give the mariachis the money without even kissing my mother's hand or waiting for her to bless me. Then we headed to Miss Rosas's home. Some boys and girls I knew were out in the street. This made me uncomfortable. They looked at me wonderingly as I led the mariachi band to Miss Rosas's home.

A block away from Miss Rosas's home I could see her father sitting on the curb reading the Juarez newspaper, *El Fronterizo.*

The sight of him made me slow down for a moment. But I got back in stride when I saw Miss Rosas herself.

She smiled and waved at me. "Hello, Amadito," she said.

"Hello, Cecilia," I said.

She looked at the mariachis, then back at me.

"Ay, Amado, you're going to serenade your girl," she said.

I didn't reply right away. Then when I was getting ready to say, "Cecilia, I came to serenade you," I saw the American man sitting in the sports car at the curb.

Miss Rosas turned to him. "I'll be right there, Johnny," she said.

husky: *Strong and rugged.*
mariachis: *Mexican street musicians.*

She patted my cheek. "I've got to run now, Amado," she said. "Have a real nice time, darling."

I looked at her silken legs as she got into the car. Everything had happened so fast I was dazed. Broken dreams made my head spin.

She was happy with him. That was obvious. She was smiling and laughing, looking forward to a good time. Why had she asked me to take her to the movies if she already had a boyfriend? Then I remembered how the other salesladies had laughed, how I had wondered why they were laughing when they couldn't even hear what we were saying. And I realized it had all been a joke; everyone had known it but me. Neither Miss Rosas nor the other salesladies had ever dreamed I would think she was serious about wanting me to take her to the movies. The American and Miss Rosas drove off. Gloomy thoughts oppressed me. They made me want to cry.

I thought some more. Emalina Uribe was the only other alternative. If we went over to Porfirio Diaz Street and serenaded her, I could go back to being a Mexican again. She was just as Mexican as I was.

Ema wasn't like the Americana at all. She wore wash dresses that fitted loosely. On Sundays she wore a shawl to church, and her mother wouldn't let her use lipstick or let her put on high heels.

But with a brother like Toro, who didn't like me anyway, such a serenade might be more dangerous than romantic.

The Mariachis of Tecalitlan were getting impatient. They had been paid to sing six songs and they wanted to sing them. But they were all sympathetic. None of them laughed at me.

"Amado, don't look sad as I did the day I learned I'd never be a millionaire," the mariachi captain said, putting his arm around me. "If not that girl, then another."

But without Miss Rosas there was no one we could sing "La Cecilia" to. The street seemed bleak and empty now that she was gone. And I didn't want to serenade Ema Uribe, even though she hadn't been faithless as Miss Rosas had been. It was true she hadn't been faithless, but only lack of opportunity would keep her from getting into a car with an American, I reasoned cynically.

Just about then Miss Rosas's father looked up from his newspaper. He asked the mariachis if they knew how to sing "Cananea Jail." They told him they did. Then they looked at me. I thought it over for a moment. Then I nodded and started strumming the bass strings of my guitar. What had happened made it only too plain I could never trust Miss Rosas again. So we serenaded her father instead.

---

oppressed: *Weighed heavily upon or depressed (op- means against).* "Gloomy thoughts" is a clue.

bleak: *Depressing.* "... empty now that she was gone" is a clue.
cynically: *Scornfully or bitterly.*

Thinking about Your Prereading Reactions

Return to the predictions you and your classmates made before you finished reading the story. With your class, decide which ones came closest to what actually happened.

Understanding Intended Meaning

Discuss the following questions with your class.

1. How does Amado feel about his job at La Feria Department Store? How do you know?

2. For what two reasons does he keep the job?

3. How does Amado spend most of his time while he is supposed to be working?

4. How does Amado interpret Cecilia Rosas's routine comments to him?

5. What "self-improvements" does he try to make in order to win her love?

6. What joke does Miss Rosas play on Amado? When does he realize what she has done?

Now read the story again before proceeding to the following activities. This time you may want to examine more carefully any details you did not fully understand during your first reading.

Making Inferences

Discuss the following questions with a small group.

1. Why is Cecilia called "La Americana"? Is this name intended to be a compliment? Explain.

2. What do you think Miss Sandoval means when she warns, "Don't go too fast with the Americana, Amado. Remember the procession is long and the candles are small" (page 79)?

3. When Amado leaves to serenade Cecilia, he leaves the house "without even kissing [his] mother's hand or waiting for her to bless [him]" (page 81). Do these actions mean he does not love her anymore? Explain.

4. Amado reports, "Sometimes I went to the men's room and looked at myself in the mirror for as long as ten minutes at a time. Such self-studies filled me with gloom. Only my hair gave me hope" (page 78). What does this tell you about his self-image? Are there other lines in the story that give you a similar message?

5. Which parts of the story seem humorous to you? Do you think the author intended them to be funny? Which parts do you find a bit sad? Explain.

Discovering the Character

Try to learn as much as you can about Cecilia Rosas. Consider how she might describe herself, how Amado describes her, and how the other salesladies describe her. Complete the following columns.

How she might describe herself	How Amado describes her	How the other sales-ladies describe her
more American than Mexican		

How would you describe Cecilia Rosas? Write a few sentences about her.

_____

_____

_____

_____

Which of the descriptions in the three columns above comes closest to your own description? Compare your work with that of a classmate. You may want to make changes based on what you learn.

Relating to Self

Discuss two or more of the following questions with a partner.

1. Is what Amado feels for Cecilia really "love"? Explain. Have you ever felt this way about someone? In what ways were your thoughts, dreams, and actions similar to those of Amado? In what ways were they different? How old were you at the time? What eventually happened to the relationship?

2. Amado's uncle laughs at the thought of a young teenager going out with a twenty-year-old woman. How important do you think age differences are in dating for teenagers? For adults? Explain.

3. Why do you think Cecilia plays a joke on Amado? How do you feel about people who play such jokes?

4. How did Amado react to the joke? How would you have reacted if you were Amado? What do you think Amado learned from this experience other than that he "could never trust Miss Rosas again" (page 82)? Explain.

5. What kinds of things seem important to the characters in the story? Good looks? Dressing right? Being a trusted friend? Anything else? How do their values differ from one another's? Do you think their values will change over time? Explain. How close do their values come to your own?

Comparing Cultural Expectations

Discuss one or more of the following questions with a small group.

1. Cecilia advises Amado to "speak English. And pronounce the words slowly and carefully, so you don't sound like a country Mexican" (page 79). Does being "American" mean you shouldn't speak your first language? Explain. What about changing your name, as Cecilia has done, or changing your eating habits, as Amado wants to do? How might your family react if you tried to do such things? Would their reactions be similar to those of Amado's family? Why or why not?

2. To what extent is it possible to keep one's first language and culture when moving to a new place where the language and culture are very different? Think about what Diana Chang reveals to us in the poem on page 75.

3. What advice would you give a person who is planning to become part of another culture? Consider what you have learned from this unit, from other units in this book, and from your own knowledge and experience.

Detecting Foreshadowing in the Story

Authors usually prepare their readers with very small hints about what is going to happen in a story. Otherwise, the readers might not believe the events when they occur. This technique is called *foreshadowing*. In this story, we find that Amado's expected date with Cecilia Rosas has been a joke all along. When we look back in the story, we see that there were hints of this possibility. For example, Miss Sandoval's warning serves as a hint that the story may not turn out exactly the way Amado thinks it will. What other bits of foreshadowing can you find that might lead you to believe that Cecilia is not seriously interested in dating Amado? Discuss your ideas with your class and the teacher.

Reading Critically

The story "Cecilia Rosas" first appeared in *The New Mexico Quarterly* in 1964. In what ways do you think the story would be different if it were written today? For example, would serenading be used as a way to win someone's love? Would a boy take dance lessons to impress a girl? What about the values which seemed to be important to Amado and Cecilia? Would those still be important values today? Discuss your ideas with a small group.

Developing Your Word Bank

Many of the more common words and phrases used in this unit reappear in other selections throughout the book. List in your Word Bank (see page 152) a few of the words or phrases that are new to you. Choose only those words or phrases that you feel will be useful. You may want to work with a partner or have your teacher help you with this task. Consider words you might want to use in conversation, in writing, or in communication about an academic area in which you have a special interest.

Ideas for Discussion and/or Writing

Choose one or more of the following activities.

1. Are you learning English in a country where it is a commonly used language? If so, write several questions to ask fluent speakers of English. Following are a few sample questions:

   ◆ Have you ever been between two cultures? If so, what were the two cultures?
   ◆ What was it like for you to be between two cultures? What were the problems? Were there any advantages?
   ◆ Were there times when you were fearful? Explain.
   ◆ How did you overcome the problems involved in being between two cultures?

   Interview several people outside your class. After each interview, write down what you can remember of the answers you received. Share a few of the more interesting answers with your class.

2. Write your own story or poem based on your experiences of being between two cultures. Be sure to include descriptive language. If you write a story, you will also want to include foreshadowing. You and your classmates may want to put together a collection of your stories and poems to share with others.

3. Bring to class an item from or about the culture you know best that is your favorite or makes you very proud. It can be a story, poem, song, piece of art (or photo of one), or any other item that you might want to share with a small group. In what ways does this particular item make you happy to be part of the culture from which it comes?

4. Independently or with a partner, write a different ending to the story by Amado Muro. Begin with the line "Friday came at last" (see page 80). Share your ending with the class. You and your classmates might want to act out a few of the endings.

Notes

1. New England refers to the northeastern United States, and includes Connecticut, Maine, Massachusetts, New Hampshire, Rhode Island, and Vermont.
2. Amadito is a familiar or endearing form of Amado.

UNIT 7

THE SEARCH FOR LOVE

Many people place a great deal of importance on love—on finding love and then, once it's found, on keeping it. Some people are very successful in their attempts. Others can never seem to bring love within their grasp. Why do you think some people are successful at love and others are not? Discuss with your class.

In the search for love, people sometimes experience relationships that leave them hurt or angry. Such people may purposely close themselves off to love's possibilities. The following song has a message for people who may have, for one reason or another, sealed themselves against love.

The Rose

Amanda McBroom

Some say love it is a river
that drowns the tender reed.
Some say love it is a razor,
that leaves your soul to bleed.
Some say love it is a hunger
an endless aching need.
I say love it is a flower
and you its only seed.
It's the heart afraid of breaking
that never learns to dance.
It's the dream afraid of waking
that never takes the chance.
It's the one who won't be taken
who cannot seem to give,
and the soul afraid of dyin'
that never learns to live.
When the night has been too lonely
and the road has been too long,
and you think that love is only
for the lucky and the strong,
just remember in the winter
far beneath the bitter snows
lies the seed that with the sun's love
in the spring becomes the rose.

Determining the Main Idea

In your own words, write a statement that you think expresses the main idea of the song. Compare your statement with that of a partner. Discuss any difference in opinion you may have, using words from the song to support your point of view.

_____

_____

_____

Relating to Self

Discuss the following with a partner.

In the first half of the song, love is compared to several things: a river, a razor, a hunger, a flower. Discuss the meaning of each comparison. With which one do you most agree? Why?

Appreciating Descriptive Language

Discuss the following questions with your class.

1. *Symbolism* is another type of descriptive language. In literature a symbol is an idea or concept used to represent another idea or concept. For example, a solid gold necklace might symbolize greed or a tree might symbolize all of life.

    Look again at the song "The Rose." Do you see any symbolism in the words "just remember in the winter far beneath the bitter snows lies the seed that with the sun's love in the spring becomes the rose"? Consider especially the words "bitter snows," "the seed," "the spring," and "the rose." What clues from the song lead you to your conclusions?

2. Does the use of symbolism increase your enjoyment of this song? Why or why not?

chủ nghĩa tượng trưng

It is not unusual for people to have many misconceptions about love and what makes it thrive. Read the following statements. Check the ones you think are true.

    a. When you feel that the romance has left your relationship, it is time to move on to a new relationship with another person.

    b. It is a bad sign when one partner in a love relationship wants to make changes in the relationship itself.

    c. A strong physical attraction for one's partner is necessary in order for a love relationship to blossom.

    d. In a lasting relationship, partners have enough in common that they don't need outside activities with other people to lead happy, fulfilling lives.

    e. Conflict should be avoided if one wants a love relationship to last.

Now read the following essay. After you read it, you will be asked to look back at your answers to this activity to see if you still feel the same way.

The authors of the following essay attempt to define romance and love—what they are and how they relate to one another. The authors also give a warning. See if you agree with their conclusions.

from **Romantic Deceptions and Reality**

Dr. Stanley J. Katz and Aimee E. Liu

Romance can be dangerously seductive. A moonlit night, a crackling fire—and the mood is complete. Add an attractive partner and some soft background music, and who can resist feeling "in love"? This, after all, is what the magazine ads say love is supposed to look like. If you find a partner who provides this setting and invites you in, it's natural to think of love.

Romance is both an atmosphere and a state of mind. It's easy to bask in it and feel great for awhile. However, no long-term relationship can remain always romantic. Ideally, romance will be woven through a loving relationship, and reviving it now and then is an excellent way to express affection and commitment. But romance on demand and romance that is taken for granted are not really romantic. If you insist that your relationship be in a constant state of romance, not only are you asking the impossible but this pressure may end up destroying your chances for success as a truly loving couple.

One compelling reason for the power of romance, however, is that it momentarily satisfies one's yearnings to be adored and to escape from routine. Everyone wants to be prized from time to time—to feel special and to be reassured that others recognize one's qualities. When someone goes to a great deal of trouble (or what seems a great deal of trouble) to set just the right mood, give you just what you want, and treat you as if you were special, you naturally are pleased—and, understandably, you may confuse this pleasure with love.

As unromantic as it may seem, true love revolves around shared goals and commitment more than around passion. This is not to say that passion is absent in genuine love, but it fades in and out. When it decreases, lovers make the active choice to continue giving each other affection, encouragement, support, and attention. In genuine love there's a balance between mutual supportiveness and independence. Change and personal growth challenge the relationship instead of threatening it. Lack of change is viewed as a warning sign that the relationship is too tight. Because both partners are committed to loving each other and understand that this balance is an important part of true love, they can accept the challenges that arise. False love's greatest downfall is that it retreats from problems instead of facing them.

All of this does not mean that romantic behavior automatically should be suspect. It's natural to expect to achieve some level of romance in a new relationship. That's part of what makes a relationship fun and exciting. But it's necessary that both partners understand the role that romance is playing.

---

seductive: *Powerfully tempting (se- means apart or away from; -duc-means to lead). The next two sentences offer clues.*
bask: *Enjoy the warmth.*
reviving: *Bringing back to life (re- means again; -viv- refers to life).*
commitment: *Here it means the acceptance of certain responsibilities regarding another person (com- means together; -mit- means to send or put).*
taken for granted: *Assumed to always be available.*
compelling: *Irresistible or forceful (com- means together; -pel- means drive or force).*

yearnings: *Desires. ". . . to be adored and to escape from routine" is a clue.*
revolves: *Moves in a circle (re- here means back; -volve- refers to rolling). ". . . around shared goals and commitment" is a clue.*
mutual: *Felt or shared equally by two or more people.*
retreats: *Backs away. ". . . from problems instead of facing them" is a clue.*
suspect: *(pronounced here "sǎ-spekt"). Here it means doubted.*

In true love, the purpose of romance is not to deceive but to express genuine affection and enrich an ongoing relationship. It is heartfelt. It pleases both partners and renews their commitment to each other. It gives them a brief break from the daily grind, an opportunity to focus on each other and the relationship in a positive way.

Once you've determined that you and your partner both are prepared to accept true love, you need to make sure the ties are there to hold the two of you together as a couple. These strengths will form the base for your love, supporting your relationship through the challenges to come. They fall into the following eight general categories:

1. Physical attraction. The attraction need not be electric. With many loving couples, it builds gradually and gently, sometimes taking years to ripen. All that's really required in the beginning is some attraction, mutual openness, affection, and desire for intimacy.

2. Shared goals, interests, and belief systems. Couples with similar religious, ethnic, and political beliefs tend to be more united than those with differing backgrounds, but differences can be overcome if the mesh of goals and other interests is strong.

3. Mutual respect, acceptance, and the desire to please each other. In relationships based on false love, these attitudes often flow from one partner only. The wife may honor her husband, for example, while he treats her with scorn. In true love, there must be balance, and both partners must accept the responsibility of living up to each other's expectations.

4. Mutual honesty and trust. Deceit has no place in true love. It breeds mistrust and division. At the outset, you and your partner must be truthful, both with yourselves and with each other.

5. Realistic expectations for each other and the relationship. Your expectations should be based both on the requirements for true love and on your individual personalities and needs. Discuss them openly, recognizing that some are nonnegotiable while others need to remain flexible.

6. A balance of dependence and independence. True love requires a connection, but not the submersion, of two individuals. Mature lovers do not merge completely, as obsessive couples do, nor do they remain disconnected. Rather, they interlock, so that parts of their lives become shared. In diagram form, the three possibilities look like this:

 Obsessive couple    Disconnected couple    Loving couple

---

daily grind: The day-to-day routine.
intimacy: Here it means the state of physical or sexual closeness to another person.
mesh: Here it means the bringing together of.
scorn: Anger and disgust.
deceit: Falseness.
outset: Beginning.
nonnegotiable: Not capable of being changed as part of a compromise.

". . . while others need to remain flexible" is a clue.
submersion: The state of being completely covered by or under the surface of something (sub- means under).
merge: Blend together, losing individual identity.
obsessive: Having a fixed, unreasonable idea that often causes anxiety (ob- means on; -ses- refers to sitting).
interlock: Join closely together (inter- means between or among).
". . . so that parts of their lives become shared" is a clue.

To succeed in love, you and your partner must be able to rely on each other for comfort and support without expecting all your needs to be met within the relationship. Part of your life must remain separate. You need some friends, activities, and interests that your partner does not share. In addition to the personal benefits you get from these outside sources, they provide ideas, energy, and information that you bring back to keep the relationship open and developing.

7. A cooperative approach to problems. Conflict and struggle are necessary to life and therefore also to love. You and your partner must accept this fact from the outset and figure out how you will deal with problems when they arise. The process of working through difficulties should help you understand each other better and bring you closer together.

8. A shared life. True love does not occur without effort and it does not develop overnight. For most of us, it takes years to reach fulfillment. Facades fade away as defenses decrease. Through the routine of daily life, you and your partner come to know each other's secret yearnings and discover and become part of each other's inner rhythms.

Thinking about Your Prereading Reactions

Return to the statements on page 93. Look again at your reactions. Have your ideas changed now that you've read "Romantic Deceptions and Reality"? If so, think about how and why.

Understanding Intended Meaning

Discuss the following questions with your class.

1. According to the authors, what can happen if people insist that a relationship always be romantic?

2. What do the authors feel is "false love's" greatest downfall? Explain.

3. Do the authors think that all romantic behavior is dangerous? Explain.

4. Explain the balance between dependence and independence as illustrated by the circles on page 95. Do you agree with the authors' conclusions? Why or why not?

---

facades: *False fronts (faca- refers to face).*
defenses: *Things used to defend or protect.*

Now read the essay again before proceeding to the following activities. This time you may want to examine more carefully any details you did not fully understand during your first reading.

Using a Continuum to Clarify Ideas

A continuum allows the reader to more clearly see the relationship between two concepts without having to separate them completely. It often encourages a more accurate analysis because the reader does not need to force concepts into "black or white" categories, but can instead see them in varying shades of grey.

In "Romantic Deceptions and Reality," the authors distinguish two kinds of love relationships: romance and love. Toward which end of the continuum is each of the following characteristics likely to fall? Place each one somewhere along the line below. See the example.

- ◆ is dangerously seductive
- ◆ revolves around shared goals and commitment
- ◆ considers problems to be challenges
- ◆ satisfies one's yearnings to be adored
- ◆ can serve as an escape from routine
- ◆ balances mutual supportiveness and independence
- ◆ retreats from problems
- ◆ involves passion and strong physical attraction

Romance —is dangerously seductive   **Love**

Discuss your answers with a small group. Make any changes you want to based on what you learn.

Drawing Comparisons

Discuss the following questions with your class.

1. Discuss the feelings of love experienced by Amado Muro in Unit 6. If Amado had read the essay by Katz and Liu, how might it have helped him to understand his emotions?

2. In Unit 5 we learned that the "special powers" people possess may be simply an illusion. In what way might romance, as described by Katz and Liu, also be an illusion? Would it be an illusion in the same sense as special powers are? Explain.

Relating to Self

Discuss one or both of the following questions with a partner.

1. Examine the eight general categories of strengths in a relationship (see pages 95–96). How important do you think each one is? Would you change or add to any of the categories? Explain.

2. What experiences have you had with love? Relate them to what you have learned from this reading.

Comparing Cultural Expectations

Discuss the following questions with a small group.

1. Is the distinction the authors make between romance and love relevant in the culture you know best? Explain.

2. The authors stress the importance of commitment. What do you think they mean by commitment? Does commitment mean the same thing in the culture you know best? Explain.

Love is a common theme throughout Western literature. It has even become the subject of many cartoons, such as the ones below. With a small group discuss each cartoon and the message that it presents.

SINGLE SLICES cartoons by Peter Kohlsaat, copyright © Los Angeles Times Syndicate. Reprinted with permission

LUANN CARTOON by Greg Evans, reprinted with special permission of North American Syndicate.

horoscope: *Predictions about a person's future based on the positions of the planets and stars at a given time (horo- means hour; a scope is a means of observation).*

Virgo: *One of the many signs of the zodiac. The zodiac is a diagram showing the imaginary paths of the planets. People born between August 23 and September 22 are said to be Virgos.*

The following poem expresses a very positive view of love and what it can be. Think about love as you have experienced it. How does your attitude toward love compare with the attitude described here?

from The Prophet
Kahlil Gibran

Love one another but make not a bond of love:

Let it rather be a moving sea between the shores of your souls.

Fill each other's cup but drink not from one cup.

Give one another your bread but eat not from the same loaf.

Sing and dance together and be joyous, but let each one of you be alone,

Even as the strings of a lute are alone though they quiver with the same musi

Give your hearts, but not into each others keeping.

For the hand of life can contain your hearts.

And stand together, yet not too near together:

For the pillars of the temple stand apart,

And the oak tree and the cypress grow not in each other's shadow.

Understanding Intended Meaning

Discuss the following questions with your class.

1. What basic advice does the poet give to lovers? Try to restate his advice in your own words.

2. To what things does the poet compare lovers? Explain how each comparison supports the poet's message.

3. Is the message of this poem similar to the message of the essay by Katz and Liu? Note in particular the illustrations on page 95.

4. What do you think Gibran means by "the hand of life"?

prophet: *One who predicts the future (pro- means before).*
lute: *A musical instrument that is pear-shaped and has strings.*
quiver: *To shake rapidly or vibrate.*
pillars: *Columns used for support.*

oak tree: *A tree bearing acorns (a type of nut).*
cypress: *An evergreen tree with very small needles. It grows in warm climates.*

Relating to Self

Do you agree with the advice Gibran gives to lovers in this poem? How well do your own experiences support his ideas? Discuss your opinions with a partner.

Developing Your Word Bank

Many of the more common words and phrases used in this unit reappear in other selections throughout the book. List in your Word Bank (see page 152) a few of the words or phrases that are new to you. Choose only those words or phrases that you feel will be useful. You may want to work with a partner or have your teacher help you with this task. Consider words you might want to use in conversation, in writing, or in communication about an academic area in which you have a special interest.

Ideas for Discussion and/or Writing

Choose one or more of the following activities.

1. Find a song, poem, story, essay, or cartoon about love. Share it with a small group. Tell your group why you find this particular piece meaningful. Your class may want to put several of the pieces together in a collection for others to read.

2. Look again at the categories identified by Dr. Stanley J. Katz and Aimee E. Liu on pages 95–96. Which one do you feel is the most important? Use it as a topic for a short essay of your own. Share your essay with a partner. Ask your partner to write a brief response, including areas of agreement or disagreement. You may want to react in writing to your partner's response, thus continuing the discussion in writing.

3. Do you know of a couple who seem to be especially happy? Describe their relationship. Why do you think it is successful? Share your thoughts with at least one other person.

4. Interview one or two family members or friends outside of your class to learn about their attitudes toward love. Write several questions to ask. Following are a few examples.

   ◆ Why are some love relationships highly successful? Why do others fail?
   ◆ What do you feel is the most important requirement in a good love relationship?
   ◆ What qualities do you think are important in a partner?

   After each interview, write down what you can remember about the answers you received. Share a few of the more interesting answers with members of your class.

UNIT 8

SURVIVAL

Struggles for survival are common to all living things. The field mouse tries to escape the claws of a cat searching for food; the small fish scatter to avoid the shark's teeth; the pigeon flies from the hawk. For humans, the struggles are usually more varied. Whereas physical struggles often involve life-or-death results, everyday struggles are more likely to involve psychological (mental) or social matters—such as the struggle for independence, power, respect, or love. What kinds of struggles for survival have you experienced in your own life or heard or read about? Share these experiences with a small group.

from To Build a Fire

Jack London

Here, Jack London writes of a man and his traveling companion, a dog, who begin a journey in the extremely cold Klondike area of Canada. The man, who is a newcomer to the area, is looking forward to joining his friends (he calls them "boys") at a camp several miles away. As this part of the story opens, the man recalls advice about such journeys given to him by an old-timer from a place called Sulfur Creek—advice that he comes to wish he had listened to more carefully.

. . . It certainly was cold, was his thought. That man from Sulfur Creek had spoken the truth when telling how cold it sometimes got in the country. And he had laughed at him at the time! That showed one must not be too sure of things. There was no mistake about it, it was cold. He strode up and down, stamping his feet and threshing his arms, until reassured by the returning warmth. Then he got out matches and proceeded to make a fire. From the undergrowth, where high water of the previous spring had lodged a supply of seasoned twigs, he got his firewood. Working carefully from a small beginning, he soon had a roaring fire, over which he thawed the ice from his face and in the protection of which he ate his biscuits. For the moment the cold of space was outwitted. The dog took satisfaction in the fire, stretching out close enough for warmth and far enough away to escape being singed.

Jack London, who lived from 1876 to 1916, was a famous American writer of short stories and novels. He himself was no stranger to physical struggles for survival. He began as a homeless child in Oakland, California, and spent many years roaming across the United States and Canada. *The Call of the Wild, White Fang,* and *The Sea-Wolf* are among his best-known works.

old-timer: *A person who has lived a long time.*
strode: *Walked with long steps (the past tense of* stride*).*
threshing: *Thrashing or moving wildly about.*
seasoned: *Here it means dried enough to be usable as firewood.*

biscuits: *Small cakes of bread made without yeast.*
outwitted: *Outsmarted or defeated by superior cleverness (*wit *here means intelligence).*
singed: *(pronounced "sĭnjd") Burned on the edges.*

When the man had finished, he filled his pipe and took his comfortable time over a smoke. Then he pulled on his mittens, settled the ear flaps of his cap firmly about his ears, and took the creek trail up the left fork. The dog was disappointed and yearned back toward the fire. This man did not know cold. Possibly all the generations of his ancestry had been ignorant of cold, of real cold, of cold one hundred and seven degrees below freezing point.[1] But the dog knew; all its ancestry knew, and it had inherited the knowledge. And it knew that it was not good to walk abroad in such fearful cold. It was the time to lie snug in a hole in the snow and wait for a curtain of cloud to be drawn across the face of outer space whence this cold came. On the other hand, there was no keen intimacy between the dog and the man. The one was the toil-slave of the other, and the only caresses it had ever received were the caresses of the whiplash and of harsh and menacing throat sounds that threatened the whiplash. So the dog made no effort to communicate its apprehension to the man. It was not concerned with the welfare of the man; it was for its own sake that it yearned back toward the fire. But the man whistled, and spoke to it with the sound of whiplashes, and the dog swung in at the man's heels and followed after. . . .

And then it happened. At a place where there were no signs, where the soft, unbroken snow seemed to advertise solidity beneath, the man broke through. It was not deep. He wet himself halfway to the knees before he floundered out to the firm crust.

He was angry, and cursed his luck aloud. He had hoped to get into camp with the boys at six o'clock, and this would delay him an hour, for he would have to build a fire and dry out his footgear. This was imperative at that low temperature—he knew that much; and he turned aside to the bank, which he climbed. On top, tangled in the underbrush about the trunks of several small spruce trees, was a high-water deposit of dry firewood—sticks and twigs, principally, but also larger portions of seasoned branches and fine, dry, last year's grasses. He threw down several large pieces on top of the snow. This served for a foundation and prevented the young flame from drowning itself in the snow it otherwise would melt.

The Klondike is an area which is located in the Yukon Territory of northwest Canada. Very few people live there, probably due to the harsh living conditions. Fur trapping, mining, and fishing are very important to the economy.

---

creek trail: *The trail formed by a frozen creek.*
fork: *Here it means one of the streams into which a creek is divided.*
snug: *Cozy and secure.*
whence: *An old-fashioned way to say "from where."*
keen: *Here it means strong.*
toil-slave: *Work-slave.*
caresses: *Gentle touches.*
whiplash: *A whip used to hit the dogs pulling a sled to make them run faster.*

menacing: *Threatening ". . . that threatened the whiplash" is a clue.*
solidity: *The state of being solid. ". . . unbroken snow" is a clue.*
floundered: *Moved clumsily to try to regain one's footing. ". . . out to the firm crust" is a clue.*
cursed: *Declared to be evil; swore or used profane language. "He was angry" is a clue.*
footgear: *Clothing worn on the feet.*
imperative: *Very necessary.*
spruce: *An evergreen tree having needles and cones.*

The flame he got by touching a match to a small shred of birch bark that he took from his pocket. This burned even more readily than paper. Placing it on the foundation, he fed the young flame with wisps of dry grass and with the tiniest dry twigs.

He worked slowly and carefully, keenly aware of his danger. Gradually, as the flame grew stronger, he increased the size of the twigs with which he fed it. He squatted in the snow, pulling the twigs out from their entanglement in the brush and feeding directly to the flame. He knew there must be no failure. When it is seventy-five below zero a man must not fail in his first attempt to build a fire—that is, if his feet are wet. If his feet are dry, and he fails, he can run along the trail for half a mile and restore his circulation. But the circulation of wet and freezing feet cannot be restored by running when it is seventy-five below. No matter how fast he runs, the wet feet will freeze the harder.

All this the man knew. The old-timer on Sulfur Creek had told him about it the previous fall, and now he was appreciating the advice. Already all sensation had gone out of his feet. To build the fire, he had been forced to remove his mittens, and the fingers had quickly gone numb. His pace of four miles an hour had kept his heart pumping blood to the surface of his body and to all the extremities. But the instant he stopped, the action of the pump eased downhill. Nose and cheeks were already freezing, while the skin of all his body chilled as it lost its blood.

But he was safe. Toes and nose and cheeks would be only touched by the frost, for the fire was beginning to burn with strength. He was feeding it with twigs the size of his finger. In another minute he would be able to feed it with branches the size of his wrist, and then he could remove his wet footgear, and while it dried, he could keep his naked feet warm by the fire, rubbing them at first, of course, with snow. The fire was a success. He was safe. He remembered the advice of the old-timer on Sulfur Creek, and smiled. The old-timer had been very serious in laying down the law that no man must travel alone in the Klondike after fifty below. Well, here he was; he had had the accident; he was alone; and he had saved himself. Those old-timers were rather womanish, some of them, he thought. All a man had to do was to keep his head, and he was all right. Any man who was a man could travel alone. But it was surprising the rapidity with which his cheeks and nose were freezing. And he had not thought his fingers could go lifeless in so short a time. Lifeless they were, for he could scarcely make them come together to grip a twig, and they seemed remote from his body and from him. When he touched a twig he had to look and see whether or not he had hold of it. The wires were pretty well down between him and his finger ends.

All of which counted for little. There was the fire, snapping and crackling and promising life with every dancing flame. He started to untie his moccasins. They were coated with ice; the thick German socks were like sheaths of iron halfway to the knees; and the moccasin strings were like rods of steel all twisted and knotted as by some conflagration. For a moment he tugged with his numb fingers, then, realizing the folly of it, he drew his sheath knife.

But before he could cut the strings it happened. It was his own fault, or, rather, his

---

shred: Here it means a thin strip.
birch bark: The pale or white outer covering of a birch tree.
wisps: Small fragments.
entanglement: The state of being twisted together (tangle means to intertwine in a confused mass).
circulation: Here it means the movement of blood around the body (cir- means around or circle).

sensation: Here it means bodily feeling. " . . . had gone out of his feet" is a clue.
extremities: The parts of the body that are farthest from the center; usually refers to the hands and feet (ex- means out).
sheaths: Coverings.
conflagration: A large fire.
folly: Foolishness.

mistake. He should not have built the fire under the spruce tree. He should have built it in the open. But it had been easier to pull the twigs from the bush and drop them directly on the fire. Now the tree under which he had done this carried a weight of snow on its boughs. No wind had blown for weeks, and each bough was fully freighted. Each time he had pulled a twig he had communicated a slight agitation to the tree—an imperceptible agitation, so far as he was concerned, but an agitation sufficient to bring about the disaster. High up in the tree one bough capsized its load of snow. This fell on the boughs beneath, capsizing them. This process continued spreading out and involving the whole tree. It grew like an avalanche, and it descended without warning upon the man and the fire, and the fire was blotted out! Where it had burned was a mantle of fresh and disordered snow.

The man was shocked. It was as though he had just heard his own sentence of death. For a moment he sat and stared at the spot where the fire had been. Then he grew very calm. Perhaps the old-timer on Sulfur Creek was right. If he had only had a trailmate he would have been in no danger now. The trailmate could have built the fire. Well, it was up to him to build the fire over again, and this second time there must be no failure. Even if he succeeded, he would most likely lose some toes. His feet must be badly frozen by now, and there would be some time before the second fire was ready.

Such were his thoughts, but he did not sit and think them. He was busy all the time they were passing through his mind. He made a new foundation for a fire, this time in the open, where no treacherous tree could blot it out. Next he gathered dry grasses and tiny twigs from the high-water flotsam. He could not bring his fingers together to pull them out, but he was able to gather them by the handful. In this way he got many rotten twigs and bits of green moss that were undesirable, but it was the best he could do. He worked methodically, even collecting an armful of the larger branches to be used later when the fire gathered strength. And all the while the dog sat and watched him, a certain yearning wistfulness in its eyes, for it looked upon him as the fire provider, and the fire was slow in coming.

When all was ready, the man reached in his pocket for a second piece of birch bark. He knew the bark was there, and though he could not feel it with his fingers, he could hear its crisp rustling as he fumbled for it. Try as he would, he could not clutch hold of it. And all the while the dog sat in the snow, its wolf brush of a tail curled around warmly over its forefeet, its sharp wolf ears pricked forward intently as it watched the man. And the man, as he beat and threshed with his arms and hands, felt a great surge of envy as he regarded the creature that was warm and secure in its natural covering.

After a time he was aware of the first faraway signals of sensation in his beaten fingers. The faint tingling grew stronger till it evolved into a stinging ache that was excruciating, but which the man hailed with satisfaction. He stripped the

---

boughs: (pronounced "bouz") Large branches of a tree.
fully freighted: Carrying as much as it could hold; loaded (freight usually refers to goods carried commercially).
agitation: Disturbance.
imperceptible: Not noticeable (im- means not; -cep- refers to seizing or grasping).
capsized: Overturned. ". . . its load of snow" is a clue.
avalanche: A large mass of falling snow. ". . . it descended without warning" is a clue.
blotted out: Gotten rid of; destroyed.
mantle: A cover.

sentence of death: A pronouncement that one must die for something one has done or failed to do.
treacherous: Very dangerous; misleading (treach- refers to trick).
flotsam: Here it means pieces of wood drifting together.
methodically: In a regular or systematic order (a method is a set of orderly procedures).
wistfulness: The state of being wishful.
forefeet: Front feet (fore- means front).
pricked: Here it means made to stand up.
surge: Here it means a sudden rush from inside (sur- means up from below).
excruciating: Extremely painful. ". . . stinging ache" is a clue.
hailed: Greeted.

mitten from his right hand and fetched forth the birch bark. The exposed fingers were quickly going numb again. Next he brought out his bunch of sulfur matches. But the tremendous cold had already driven the life out of his fingers. In his effort to separate one match from the others, the whole bunch fell in the snow. He tried to pick it out of the snow, but failed. The dead fingers could neither touch nor clutch. He was very careful. He drove the thought of his freezing feet, and nose, and cheeks, out of his mind, devoting his whole soul to the matches. He watched, using the sense of vision in place of that of touch, and when he saw his fingers on each side of the bunch, he closed them—that is, he willed to close them, for the wires were down, and the fingers did not obey. He pulled the mitten on the right hand, and beat it fiercely against his knee. Then, with both mittened hands, he scooped the bunch of matches, along with much snow, into his lap. Yet he was no better off.

After some manipulation he managed to get the bunch between the heels of his mittened hands. In this fashion he carried it to his mouth. The ice crackled and snapped when by a violent effort he opened his mouth. He drew the lower jaw in, curled the upper lip out of the way, and scraped the bunch with his upper teeth in order to separate a match. He succeeded in getting one, which he dropped on his lap. He was not better off. He could not pick it up. Then he devised a way. He picked it up in his teeth and scratched it on his leg. Twenty times he scratched before he succeeded in lighting it. As it flamed he held it with his teeth to the birch bark.

But the burning brimstone went up his nostrils and into his lungs, causing him to cough spasmodically. The match fell into the snow and went out.

The old-timer on Sulfur Creek was right, he thought in the moment of controlled despair that ensued: after fifty below, a man should travel with a partner. He beat his hands, but failed in exciting any sensation. Suddenly he bared both hands removing the mittens with his teeth. He caught the whole bunch of matches between the heels of his hands. His arm muscles, not being frozen, enabled him to press the hand heels tightly against the matches. Then he scratched the bunch along his leg. It flared into flame, seventy sulfur matches at once! There was no wind to blow them out. He kept his head to one side to escape the strangling fumes, and held the blazing bunch to the birch bark. As he so held it, he became aware of sensation in his hand. His flesh was burning. He could smell it. Deep down below the surface he could feel it. The sensation developed into pain that grew acute. And still he endured it, holding the flame of the matches clumsily to the bark that would not light readily because his own burning hands were in the way, absorbing most of the flame.

At last, when he could endure no more, he jerked his hands apart. The blazing matches fell sizzling into the snow, but the birch bark was alight. He began laying dry grasses and the tiniest twigs on the flame. He could not pick and choose, for he had to lift the fuel between the heels of his hands. Small pieces of rotten wood and green moss clung to the twigs, and he bit them off as well as he could with his teeth. He

---

fetched forth: Brought forward or into view.
sulfur: A yellow chemical used to make matches.
willed: Here it means wanted.
wires: Here it refers to the connections between the brain and the fingers.
manipulation: Here it means the act of using one's hands skillfully (man- means hand).
devised: Planned or invented.

spasmodically: In uncontrollable bursts or spasms, which are sudden muscle contractions.
ensued: Followed (en- here means onward).
acute: Here it means sharp (acu- refers to a needle or point).
endured: Continued to bear.
alight: An old-fashioned way of saying lit up.
cherished: Held dear or treasured.

cherished the flame carefully and awkwardly. It meant life, and it must not perish. The withdrawal of blood from the surface of his body now made him begin to shiver, and he grew more awkward. A large piece of green moss fell squarely on the little fire. He tried to poke it out with his fingers, but his shivering frame made him poke too far, and he disrupted the nucleus of the little fire, the burning grasses and tiny twigs separating and scattering. He tried to poke them together again, but, in spite of the tenseness of the effort, his shivering got away with him, and the twigs were hopelessly scattered. Each twig gushed a puff of smoke and went out. The fire provider had failed. As he looked apathetically about him, his eyes chanced on the dog, sitting across the ruins of the fire from him, in the snow, making restless, hunching movements, slightly lifting one forefoot and then the other, shifting its weight back and forth on them with wistful eagerness.

The sight of the dog put a wild idea into his head. He remembered the tale of the man, caught in a blizzard, who killed a steer and crawled inside the carcass, and so was saved. He would kill the dog and bury his hands in the warm body until the numbness went out of them. Then he could build another fire. He spoke to the dog, calling it to him; but in his voice was a strange note of fear that frightened the animal, who had never known the man to speak in such a way before. Something was the matter, and its suspicious nature sensed danger—it knew not what danger, but somewhere, somehow, in its brain arose an apprehension of the man. It flattened its ears down at the sound of the man's voice, and its restless, hunching movements and the liftings and shiftings of its forefeet became more pronounced; but it would not come to the man. He got on his hands and knees and crawled toward the dog. This unusual posture again excited suspicion, and the animal sidled mincingly away.

The man sat up in the snow for a moment and struggled for calmness. Then he pulled on his mittens, by means of his teeth, and got upon his feet. He glanced down at first in order to assure himself that he was really standing up, for the absence of sensation in his feet left him unrelated to the earth. His erect position in itself started to drive the webs of suspicion from the dog's mind; and when he spoke peremptorily with the sound of whiplashes in his voice, the dog rendered its customary allegiance and came to him. As it came within reaching distance, the man lost his control. His arms flashed out to the dog, and he experienced genuine surprise when he discovered that his hands could not clutch, that there was neither bend nor feeling in the fingers. He had forgotten for the moment that they were frozen and that they were freezing more and more. All this happened quickly, and before the animal could get away, he encircled its body with his arms. He sat down in the snow, and in this fashion held the dog, while it snarled and whined and struggled.

But it was all he could do, hold its body encircled in his arms and sit there. He realized that he could not kill the dog. There was no way to do it. With his helpless hands he could neither draw nor hold his sheath knife nor

---

squarely: Here it means directly. ". . . on the little fire" is a clue.
nucleus: The center.
gushed: Forced out in a sudden burst. ". . . a puff of smoke" is a clue.
apathetically: Without emotion or interest (a- here means without; -pathe- refers to feeling).
hunching: Bending over or squatting.
blizzard: A severe snowstorm.
steer: A type of ox.
carcass: A dead body.
apprehension: Dread or fear.

pronounced: Here is means noticeable.
sidled: Moved sideways.
mincingly: Here it means walking with short steps (min- refers to small).
peremptorily: Here it means commandingly. ". . . with the sound of whiplashes in his voice" is a clue.
rendered: Gave back; yielded.
allegiance: Loyalty.
throttle: Here it means choke.

throttle the animal. He released it, and it plunged wildly away, with tail between its legs, and still snarling. It halted forty feet away and surveyed him curiously, with ears sharply pricked forward. The man looked down at his hands in order to locate them, and found them hanging on the ends of his arms. It struck him as curious that one should have to use his eyes in order to find out where his hands were. He began threshing his arms back and forth, beating the mittened hands against his sides. He did this for five minutes, violently, and his heart pumped enough blood up to the surface to put a stop to his shivering. But no sensation was aroused in the hands. He had an impression that they hung like weights on the ends of his arms, but when he tried to run the impression down, he could not find it.

A certain fear of death, dull and oppressive, came to him. This fear quickly became poignant as he realized that it was no longer a mere matter of freezing his fingers and toes, or of losing his hands and feet, but that it was a matter of life and death, with the chances against him. This threw him into a panic, and he turned and ran up the creek bed along the old dim trail. The dog joined in behind and kept up with him. He ran blindly, without intention, in fear such as he had never known in his life. Slowly, as he plowed and floundered through the snow, he began to see things again—the banks of the creek, the old timber jams, the leafless aspens, and the sky. The running made him feel better. He did not shiver. Maybe, if he ran on, his feet would thaw out; and, anyway, if he ran far enough, he would reach the camp and the boys. Without doubt he would lose some fingers and toes and some of his face; but the boys would take care of him, and save the rest of him when he got there. And at the same time there was another thought in his mind that said he would never get to the camp and the boys; that it was too many miles away,

plunged: *Moved suddenly and with much force.*
surveyed: *Looked over carefully.*
curious: *Here it means odd or unexpected.*

poignant: *(pronounced "pōin´-yənt") Keenly or intensely felt.*
jams: *Crowded masses.*
aspens: *Fast-growing whitish colored trees with shiny leaves.*

that the freezing had too great a start on him, and that he would soon be stiff and dead. This thought he kept in the background and refused to consider. Sometimes it pushed itself forward and demanded to be heard, but he thrust it back and strove to think of other things. . . .

It struck him as curious that he could run at all on feet so frozen that he could not feel them when they stuck the earth and took the weight of his body. He seemed to himself to skim along above the surface, and to have no connection with the earth. Somewhere he had once seen a winged Mercury,[2] and he wondered if Mercury felt as he felt when skimming over the earth.

His theory of running until he reached camp and the boys had one flaw in it: he lacked the endurance. Several times he stumbled, and finally he tottered, crumpled up, and fell. When he tried to rise, he failed. He must sit and rest, he decided, and next time he would merely walk and keep on going. As he sat and regained his breath, he noted that he was feeling quite warm and comfortable. He was not shivering, and it even seemed that a warm glow had come to his chest and trunk. And yet, when he touched his nose or cheeks, there was no sensation. Running would not thaw them out. Nor would it thaw out his hands and feet. Then the thought came to him that the frozen portions of his body must be extending. He tried to keep this thought down, to forget it, to think of something else; he was aware of the panicky feeling that it caused, and he was afraid of the panic. But the thought asserted itself, and persisted, until it produced a vision of his body totally frozen. This was too much, and he made another wild run along the

trail. Once he slowed down to a walk, but the thought of the freezing extending itself made him run again.

And all the time the dog ran with him, at his heels. When he fell down a second time, it curled its tail over its forefeet and sat in front of him, facing him, curiously eager and intent. The warmth and security of the animal angered him, and he cursed it till it flattened down its ears appeasingly. This time the shivering came more quickly upon the man. He was losing in his battle with the frost. It was creeping into his body from all sides. The thought of it drove him on, but he ran no more than a hundred feet, when he staggered and pitched headlong. It was his last panic. When he had recovered his breath and control he sat up and entertained in his mind the conception of meeting death with dignity. However, the conception did not come to him in such terms. His idea of it was that he had been making a fool of himself, running around like a chicken with its head cut off—such was the simile that occurred to him. Well, he was bound to freeze anyway, and he might as well take it decently. With this newfound peace of mind came the first glimmerings of drowsiness. A good idea, he thought, to sleep off to death. It was like taking an anesthetic. Freezing was not so bad as people thought. There were lots worse ways to die.

He pictured the boys finding his body the next day. Suddenly he found himself with them, coming along the trail and looking for himself. And, still with them, he came around a turn in the trail and found himself lying in the snow. . . .

---

strove: *Worked hard toward some goal (the past tense of* strive*).*
skim: *To move swiftly over a surface, barely touching it.*
tottered: *Lost balance.*
crumpled up: *Collapsed.*
merely: *Only.*
extending: *Here it means spreading out (ex- means out; -tend- refers to stretching).*
asserted: *Came forward boldly.*
persisted: *Stood firm (-sist- refers to standing firm).*
appeasingly: *In an attempt to bring peace or to soothe.*

staggered: *Moved unsteadily from side to side.*
pitched headlong: *Fell swiftly, head first.*
entertained: *Here it means held in one's mind to think about carefully (enter- means between; -tain- refers to holding).*
conception: *Here it means idea or concept.*
dignity: *Self-respect.*
simile: *A comparison using the word* like *or as.*
bound to: *Here it means very likely to.*
glimmerings: *Indications (glim- means a source of light).*
anesthetic: *A substance that makes one less sensitive to pain.*

Then the man drowsed off into what seemed to him the most comfortable and satisfying sleep he had ever known. The dog sat facing him and waiting. The brief day drew to a close in a long, slow twilight. There were no signs of a fire to be made, and, besides, never in the dog's experience had it known a man to sit like that in the snow and make no fire. As the twilight drew on, its eager yearning for the fire mastered it, and with a great lifting and shifting of forefeet, it whined softly, then flattened its ears down in anticipation of being chidden by the man. But the man remained silent. Later, the dog whined loudly. And still later it crept close to the man and caught the scent of death. This made the animal bristle and back away. A little longer it delayed, howling under the stars that leaped and danced and shone brightly in the cold sky. Then it turned and trotted up the trail in the direction of the camp it knew, where were the other food providers and fire providers.

Thinking about Your Prereading Reactions

Return to the question you were asked to think about on page 103. Were the experiences you shared with a small group similar in any way to those experienced by the man in Jack London's story?

Understanding Intended Meaning

Discuss the following questions with your class.

1. Describe the weather. How do the man and the dog differ in their attitudes toward the weather?

2. What is the relationship between the man and the dog? Is it an intimate one? Explain.

3. What happens that complicates the man's situation and makes him more fully realize the danger he is in? What does he try to do about it? Is he successful? What shocks him?

4. What advice was given by the old-timer from Sulfur Creek? How does the man react to this advice at first? Does his attitude toward the advice change as the story progresses? Explain.

5. Why does the man envy the dog? (See page 107.) What does the man try to do to the dog? How does the dog react?

---

twilight: *the soft, dim light that fills the sky after sunset (twi- here means half).*
chidden: *Scolded. Chided is a more widely used word meaning the same thing.*

bristle: *Cause one's hair to stand up or become erect.*
trotted: *Moved at a fast pace between walking and running.*

6. At what point in the story does the man realize that he may actually lose his life? Describe his feelings.

7. How does the man react to his own coming death?

Now read the story again before proceeding to the following activities. This time you may want to examine more carefully any details you did not fully understand during your first reading.

Drawing Comparisons

Discuss the following questions with your class.

1. How does the relationship between the man and the dog in this story differ from the one between the man and the dog in "The Red Dog" (see Unit 3)? Are the two relationships similar in any ways?

2. Why do you think the dog was able to survive, while the man was not? Might the story have ended differently had there been a different kind of relationship between the two? Explain.

3. The man refers to the old-timers who give advice as "womanish" (see page 106). What statement is he really making about how men and women differ? What is your reaction to his implications?

Tracking the Plot of a Story

You learned in Unit 3 that the plot of a story consists of the chain of events which occur. Each event is important to the meaning of the story. In the space below, list the main events in the story by Jack London. The first one is provided for you. Discuss your list with your class and the teacher.

The Plot

1. The man and the dog are on a journey to the camp where the man is supposed to meet his friends.

_____

_____

_____

_____

_____

_____

_____

_____

_____

_____

_____

_____

_____

_____

Exploring the Conflict

As was discussed in Unit 4, every story has a conflict that is the result of a struggle between a protagonist (who desires to reach a main goal) and an antagonist (who, either directly or indirectly, tries to stop the protagonist). You learned that the antagonist does not necessarily have to be another character or group of characters; it can be nature or an idea. You learned, too, that the high point of tension between the protagonist and the antagonist is called the *climax* and the ending is called the *resolution.* With your class and the teacher, identify the following elements from "To Build a Fire."

the protagonist: _____

the protagonist's main goal: _____

the antagonist: _____

the climax: _____

the resolution: _____

Discuss your answers with your class and the teacher.

Identifying the Point of View

Point of view was talked about in Unit 3. There you learned that stories are usually told from the point of view of the author, one of the characters, or some omniscient (all-knowing) being. From which point of view is "To Build a Fire" told? Do you think the point of view made any difference in your enjoyment of the story?

It is interesting to note that you were not told the name of the man in the story; nor did you know much about him or his past. Do you think the author may have had an important reason for giving so little information? If so, do you think the reason might be related in any way to the point of view? Discuss your ideas with your class and the teacher.

Detecting Foreshadowing in the Story

You learned in Unit 6 that foreshadowing consists of hints given by the author throughout the story to prepare the reader for what happens. In "To Build a Fire" what happens is that the man dies in spite of his desperate efforts to survive. Did this event seem believable to you? If so, what hints did the author give along the way to make this event believable? Discuss your ideas with your class and the teacher.

The short selection that follows involves several types of survival, not just physical. It tells the story of a Korean American who has won victories, first over a disease that has left him deaf and later over the problems facing almost all immigrants in their new countries and new cultures. His story is most certainly a "tribute to courage," as its title suggests.

from A Tribute to Courage
Gareth Hiebert

From the window of his office on the fifth floor of a St. Paul, Minnesota, building, South Korea was a long ways away for Dr. Steven Chough.

Forty-five years ago he had been a small boy two-and-a-half years old living in Kimchon. Back there the world suddenly had become silent when spinal meningitis[3] left him without any hearing.

Then he was at the foot of the ladder he would never stop climbing.

It was in mid-January when we met for the first time. Dr. Chough was beginning to pack his books, cleaning out his desk behind the doorway marked: "ADMINISTRATOR." For him the next rung on the ladder was always the next challenge. And now he was climbing to one more called "Director of the Center for Deaf Treatment Services" at a psychiatric hospital in Michigan.

When it was suggested that he had been planting seeds of hope in hearing-impaired people, encouraging them to live as if they could hear, he smiled and began to gesticulate in the language he knew best—the signing of letters, words and phrases.

Serving as a civilian employee while in Korea with the United States Army during the Korean War,[4] he had made a friend of an American serviceman who took the time not only to learn Korean, but to learn sign language. And young Chough learned English, which he added to the Korean and Japanese he already knew, thus becoming multilingual without ever saying a word or hearing one spoken.

One day his new friend gave him a 1952 copy of an American magazine. In it was an article about

---

tribute: *A show of respect and admiration (trib- means to give).*
administrator: *One who is in charge (ad- here means to; -minist- refers to serving).*
psychiatric: *Related to the medical treatment of mental illness (psychi- refers to the spirit or soul).*
hearing-impaired: *People who have difficulty hearing (to impair means to reduce strength or ability).*
gesticulate: *Gesture.*

signing: *Here it means using signs formed by fingers and hands to communicate ideas. Such sign language is used by the deaf and those who communicate with the deaf.*
civilian: *Relating to ordinary citizens, those not in the armed forces (civi- refers to citizen).*
multilingual: *Able to speak several languages (multi- means several; -ling- refers to language).*

Gallaudet College in Washington, D.C., the world's only liberal arts college[5] for deaf students. "I've got to go there," he had said. He had to cut through red tape, persuading Korean officials that he deserved to be given an exit visa. Finally, after five years, he received it and left on his journey by ship to the United States.

The next three rungs in Dr. Cough's ladder were marked with college degree titles: bachelor's degree, master's degree and doctorate. . . .[6] "It was," he said, "to show hearing people that deaf people could do as well as hearing people. I wanted also to be a model for deaf people—to inspire them."

As we spoke that afternoon in January, Dr. Chough would take along an award he had been given for courage in 1978. He would take his diplomas. These would hang on walls in his office in Michigan.

How many more rungs were there left to climb?

Dr. Steven Chough shrugged, smiled and shook his head. He didn't know.

---

red tape: *Massive paperwork (forms to fill out, etc.).*
diplomas: *Official papers stating the specific degree title completed.*

shrugged: *Here it means raised the shoulders to show uncertainty.*

Understanding Intended Meaning

Discuss the following questions with a small group.

1. What were Steven Chough's achievements? Which one impressed you the most? Why?
2. In what ways are Steven's achievements like the rungs on a ladder?
3. What kinds of survival (physical, psychological, or social) are included in this success story? Explain.

Relating to Personal Experience

Discuss the following questions with a partner.

Do you know of any disabled persons other than Steven Chough who have immigrated to another country? What problems did they face? Were they successful in achieving their goals? Explain.

Developing Your Word Bank

List in your Word Bank (see page 152) a few of the words or phrases from this unit that are new to you. Choose only those items that you feel will be useful. You may want to work with a partner or have your teacher help you with this task. Consider words you might want to use in conversation, in writing, or in communication about an academic area in which you have a special interest.

Ideas for Discussion and/or Writing

Choose one or more of the following activities.

1. Write your own short story of survival. You may write about one or more types of survival (physical, psychological, or social). You may want to use the Jack London story as a model. Decide from what point of view you will tell your story, what the plot and conflict will consist of, and what foreshadowing you will use to make the events believable. You and your classmates may want to put together a collection of your survival stories to share with others.

2. Write your own biographical sketch entitled "A Tribute to Courage." The subject can be a person that you know very well or one you have read about. You may want to use the selection about Steven Chough as a model. Share your paper with a partner.

3. Are you now learning English in a country where it is a commonly used language? If so, write several questions to ask fluent speakers of English. Following are a few sample questions:

   ◆ Have you ever been in a situation in which you had to survive physically? If so, describe the situation and your feelings about it.

   ◆ Do you know of anyone who showed great courage in a survival situation? Who was that person? In what way did this person show courage?

   ◆ What do you think would be the hardest thing to face?

   Interview one or two people outside your class. After each interview, write down what you can remember of the answers you received. Share a few of the more interesting answers with your class.

Notes

1. One hundred and seven degrees below the freezing point is based on the Fahrenheit thermometer scale, on which the freezing point is 32 degrees.
2. Mercury was the god of travel in Roman mythology.
3. Spinal meningitis (also known as cerebrospinal meningitis) is a disease that causes inflammation of the tissues of the brain and spinal cord. It is often fatal.
4. The Korean War was fought between North Korea and South Korea between 1950 and 1953. United Nations (mainly American) forces fought on the side of South Korea.
5. A liberal arts college is one that focuses on general education (art, history, languages, and so on) rather than on training for a specific profession.
6. College degree titles are official recognition given in the United States and elsewhere upon completion of a specific program of study. A bachelor's degree generally takes four years to complete, a master's two additional years, and a doctorate up to seven years or more.

UNIT **9**

SIMPLE PLEASURES

If you could wish for anything, what would it be? How did you come to your decision? Does your answer come closer to what Calvin thinks his tiger should wish for or to what the tiger actually chooses? Discuss with a partner.

from Gift from the Sea

Anne Morrow Lindbergh

The author of the following selections from Gift from the Sea *discovers her own simple pleasures. It is through her honest self-examination during a vacation to the beach that she finds what she values most. It is there that she faces squarely the complicated web of duties that her life has become.*

I

The shell in my hand is deserted. It once housed a whelk, a snaillike creature, and then temporarily, after the death of the first occupant, a little hermit crab, who has run away, leaving his tracks behind him like a delicate vine on the sand. He ran away, and left me his shell. It was once a protection to him. I turn the shell in my hand, gazing into the wide open door from which he made his exit. Had it become an encumbrance? Why did he run away? Did he hope to find a better home, a better mode of living? I too have run away, I realize, I have shed the shell of my life, for these few weeks of vacation.

But his shell—it is simple; it is bare, it is beautiful. Small, only the size of my thumb, its architecture is perfect, down to the finest detail. Its shape, swelling like a pear in the center, winds in a gentle spiral to the pointed apex. Its color, dull gold, is whitened by salt from the sea.

My shell is not like this, I think. How untidy it has become! Blurred with moss, knobby with barnacles, its shape is hardly recognizable any more. Surely, it had a shape once. It has a shape still in my mind. What is the shape of my life?

The shape of my life today starts with a family. I have a husband, five children and a home just beyond the suburbs of New York. I have also a craft, writing, and therefore work I want

Anne Morrow Lindbergh, an American writer, was married to Charles Lindbergh, who achieved sudden fame when he made a nonstop, solo flight between New York and Paris in 1927. Tragically, their first child was kidnapped and murdered in 1932.

---

snaillike: *Like a snail: a small, soft, slow-moving creature whose shell comes to a point. It lives on land or in water.*
occupant: *One who lives in or occupies something.*
hermit crab: *A soft-bodied crab that lives in and carries the empty shell of another animal.*
encumbrance: *A burden.*
mode: *A way of doing something.*
shed: *Here it means gotten rid of or caused to fall off.*

architecture: *The basic design of a structure.*
spiral: *A shape that circles upward around a central point (a spire is a point or the highest part). ". . . swelling like a pear in the center" is a clue.*
apex: *The highest point or the top.*
knobby: *Having knobs or large bumps sticking out.*
barnacles: *Small, hard-shelled sea animals that attach themselves to surfaces under water. "*

to pursue. The shape of my life is, of course, determined by other things: my background and childhood, my mind and its education, my conscience and its pressures, my heart and its desires. I want to give and take from my children and husband, to share with friends and community, to carry out my obligations to man and to the world, as a woman, as an artist, as a citizen. . . .

I mean to lead a simple life, to choose a simple shell I can carry easily—like a hermit crab. But I do not. I find that my frame of life does not foster simplicity. My husband and five children must make their way in the world. The life I have chosen as wife and mother entrains a whole caravan of complications. It involves food and shelter; meals, planning, marketing, bills, and making the ends meet in a thousand ways. . . . It involves clothes, shopping, laundry, cleaning, mending, letting skirts down and sewing buttons on, or finding someone else to do it. It involves friends, my husband's, my children's, my own, and endless arrangements to get together; letters, invitations, telephone calls and transportation hither and yon.

What is the answer? There is no easy answer, no complete answer. I have only clues, shells from the sea. . . .

One learns first of all in beach living the art of shedding; how little one can get along with, not how much. Physical shedding to begin with, which then mysteriously spreads into other fields. Clothes, first. Of course, one needs less in the sun. But one needs less anyway, one finds suddenly one does not need a closet-full, only a small suitcase-full. And what a relief it is! Less taking up and down of hems, less mending, and—best of all—less worry about what to wear. One finds one is shedding not only clothes—but vanity.

Next, shelter. One does not need the airtight shelter one has in winter in the North. Here I live in a bare sea-shell of a cottage. No heat, no telephone, no plumbing to speak of, no hot water, a two-burner oil stove, no gadgets to go wrong. No rugs. There were some, but I rolled them up the first day; it is easier to sweep the sand off a bare floor. But I find I don't bustle about with unnecessary sweeping and cleaning here. I am no longer aware of the dust. I have shed my Puritan[1] conscience about absolute tidiness and cleanliness. Is it possible that, too, is a material burden? No curtains. I do not need them for privacy; the pines around my house are enough protection. I want the windows open all the time, and I don't want to worry about rain. I begin to shed my Martha-like[2] anxiety about many things. Washable slipcovers, faded and old—I hardly see them. I don't worry about the impression they make on other people.

I am shedding pride. As little furniture as possible; I shall not need much. I shall ask into my shell only those friends with whom I can be completely honest. I find I am shedding hypocrisy in human relationships. What a rest that will be! The most exhausting thing in life, I have discovered, is being insincere. That is why so much of social life is exhausting; one is wearing a mask. I have shed my mask. . . .

Is my sea-shell house not ugly and bare? No, it is beautiful, my house. It is bare, of course, but the wind, the sun, the smell of the pines blow through its bareness. The unfinished beams in

---

pursue: Follow.
conscience: One's sense of right and wrong (con- refers to with; -science refers to knowing).
obligations: Duties (ob- means to; -liga- means to bind).
foster: Aid in the development of.
entrains: Pulls along (-train- refers to pulling or drawing along).
caravan: Usually a group of vehicles, people, or animals moving one behind the other.
making the ends meet: Managing to live with a limited amount of money.

hither and yon: An old-fashioned way to say near and far.
mysteriously: In a way that is full of mystery.
vanity: The state of being vain or paying too much attention to appearance.
gadgets: Small mechanical devices used for specific purposes.
bustle about: Hurry around in an excited state.
slipcovers: Protective covers that are put over furniture.
hypocrisy: Pretending to have certain beliefs or virtues (hypo- means under or incomplete). ". . . be completely honest" and ". . . being insincere" are clues.

the roof are veiled by cobwebs. They are lovely, I think, gazing up at them with new eyes; they soften the hard lines of the rafters as grey hairs soften the lines on a middle-aged face. I no longer pull out grey hairs or sweep down cobwebs. As for the walls, it is true they looked forbidding at first. I felt cramped and enclosed by their blank faces. I wanted to knock holes in them, to give them another dimension with pictures or windows. So I dragged home from the beach grey arms of driftwood, worn satin-smooth by wind and sand. I gathered trailing green vines with floppy red-tipped leaves. With these tacked to the walls and propped up in corners, I am satisfied.

II

After my week alone I have had a week of living with my sister. I will take from it one day. I shall examine it, set it before me as I have set the shells on my desk. I shall turn it around like a shell, testing and analyzing its good points. Not that my life will ever become like this day— a perfect one plucked out of a holiday week; there are no perfect lives. The relation of two sisters is not that of a man and a woman. But it can illustrate the essence of relationships. The light shed by any good relationship illuminates all relationships. And one perfect day can give clues for a more perfect life.

We wake in the same small room from the deep sleep of good children, to the soft sound of wind through the casuarina trees and the gentle sleep-breathing rhythm of waves on the shore.

We run bare-legged to the beach, which lies smooth, flat, and glistening with fresh wet shells after the night's tides. The morning swim has the nature of a blessing to me, a baptism, a rebirth to the beauty and wonder of the world. We run back tingling to hot coffee on our small back porch. Two kitchen chairs and a child's table between us fill the stoop on which we sit. With legs in the sun we laugh and plan our day.

We wash dishes lightly to no system, for there are not enough to matter. We work easily and instinctively together, not bumping into each other as we go back and forth about our tasks. We talk as we sweep, as we dry, as we put away, discussing a person or a poem or a memory. And since our communication seems more important to us than our chores, the chores are done without thinking.

And then to work, behind closed doors neither of us would want to invade. What release to write so that one forgets oneself, forgets one's companion, forgets where one is or what one is going to do next—to be drenched in work as one is drenched in sleep or in the sea. Pencils and pads and curling blue sheets alive with letters leap up on the desk. And then, pricked by hunger, we rise at last in a daze, for a late lunch. Reeling a little from our intense absorption, we come back with relief to the small chores of getting lunch, as if they were lifelines to reality— as if we had indeed almost drowned in the sea of intellectual work and welcomed the firm ground of physical action under our feet.

After an hour or so of practical jobs and errands we are ready to leave them again. Out

---

rafters: *Boards that support a roof.*
forbidding: *Unfriendly or grim. "... their blank faces" is a clue.*
dimension: *Here it means size. "... to give them another dimension" means to make them seem larger.*
propped up: *Leaned against something for support.*
plucked out: *Pulled out abruptly.*
illustrate: *Explain something by using examples (-lus- refers to light).*
essence: *The most important element that gives something its identity.*
shed: *Here it means sent forth.*
casuarina: *Trees having small scalelke leaves.*
tides: *The rising and falling of the surface levels of a body of water due*

to the forces of gravity.
stoop: *Here it means a small porch or platform.*
instinctively: *With inborn knowledge (in- means within).*
invade: *Enter by force (in- here means in; -vad- means to go). "... behind closed doors" is a clue.*
drenched: *Soaked all the way through.*
pricked: *Pierced or poked.*
daze: *The state of having dulled senses.*
reeling: *Being thrown off balance.*
absorption: *The state of being pulled into something completely. "... we come back" is a clue.*

onto the beach for the afternoon where we are swept clean of duties, of the particular, of the practical. We walk up the beach in silence, but in harmony, as the sandpipers ahead of us move like a corps of ballet dancers keeping time to some interior rhythm inaudible to us. Intimacy is blown away. Emotions are carried out to sea. We are even free of thoughts, at least of their articulation; clean and bare as whitened driftwood; empty as shells, ready to be filled up again with the impersonal sea and sky and wind. A long afternoon soaking up the outer world.

III

There are all kinds of experiences on this island, but not too many. There are all kinds of people, but not too many. The simplicity of life forces me into physical as well as intellectual or social activity. I have no car, so I bicycle for my supplies and my mail. When it is cold, I collect driftwood for my fireplace and chop it up, too. I swim instead of taking hot baths. I bury my garbage instead of having it removed by a truck. And when I cannot write a poem, I bake biscuits and feel just as pleased. Most of these physical chores would be burdens at home, where my life is crowded and schedules are tight. There I have a house full of children and I am responsible for many people's lives. Here, where there is time and space, the physical tasks are a welcome change. They balance my life in a way I find refreshing and in which I seldom feel refreshed at home. Making beds or driving to market is not as refreshing as swimming or bicycling or digging in the earth. I cannot go on burying the garbage when I get home, but I can dig in a garden; I can bicycle to the cabin where I work; and I can remember to bake biscuits on bad days.

My island selects for me socially too. Its

---

harmony: *Together in a pleasing way* (harmon- *refers to joining*).
sandpipers: *Small wading birds with long legs.*
corps: (*pronounced "kōr"*) *A group of individuals moving together in one direction. "... of ballet dancers" is a clue.*

inaudible: *Not able to be heard* (in- *here means not;* -aud- *refers to hearing*).
articulation: *Here it means the act of speaking.*
impersonal: *Not personal* (im- *here means not*).

small circumference cannot hold too many people. I see people here that I would not see at home, people who are removed from me by age or occupation. In the suburbs of a large city we tend to see people of the same general age and interests. That is why we chose the suburbs, because we have similar needs and pursuits. My island selects for me people who are very different from me—the stranger who turns out to be, in the frame of sufficient time and space, invariably interesting and enriching. I discover here what everyone has experienced on an ocean voyage or a long train ride or a temporary seclusion in a small village. Out of the welter of life, a few people are selected for us by the accident of temporary confinement in the same circle. We never would have chosen these neighbors; life chose them for us. But thrown together on this island of living, we stretch to understand each other and are invigorated by the stretching. The difficulty with big city environment is that if we select—and we must in order to live and breathe and work in such crowded conditions—we tend to select people like ourselves, a very monotonous diet. All hors d'oeuvres and no meat; or all sweets and no vegetables, depending on the kind of people we are. But however much the diet may differ between us, one thing is fairly certain: we usually select the known, seldom the strange. We tend not to choose the unknown which might be a shock or a disappointment or simply a little difficult to cope with. And yet it is the unknown with all its disappointments and surprises that is the most enriching. In so many ways this island

selects for me better than I do myself at home. When I go back will I be submerged again, not only by centrifugal activities, but by too many centripetal ones? Not only by distractions but by too many opportunities? Not only by dull people but by too many interesting ones? The multiplicity of the world will crowd in on me again with its false sense of values. Values weighed in quantity, not quality; in speed, not stillness; in noise, not silence; in words, not in thoughts; in acquisitiveness, not beauty. How shall I resist the onslaught? How shall I remain whole against the strains and stresses of "Zerrissenheit?"[3]

For the natural selectivity of the island I will have to substitute a conscious selectivity based on another sense of values—a sense of values I have become more aware of here. Island-precepts, I might call them if I could define them, signposts toward another way of living. Simplicity of living, as much as possible, to retain a true awareness of life. Balance of physical, intellectual, and spiritual life. Work without pressure. Space for significance and beauty. Time for solitude and sharing. Closeness to nature to strengthen understanding and faith in the intermittency of life: life of the spirit, creative life, and the life of human relationships. A few shells.

Island living has been a lens through which to examine my own life in the North. I must keep my lens when I go back. Little by little one's holiday vision tends to fade. I must remember to see with island eyes. The shells will remind me; they must be my island eyes.

circumference: Here it means the boundary line of an area (circum- means around).
sufficient: Enough.
invariably: Unchangingly (variable means changeable).
seclusion: The state of being apart from others or secluded.
welter: Confusion.
confinement: The state of being shut into an enclosure (con- means together; -fin- refers to a border or end). "... in the same circle" is a clue.
invigorated: Given strength or vigor.
monotonous: Without variety (mono- means one).
hors d'oeuvres: (pronounced "ôr-dûrv'-zǝ") Appetizers or fancy bits of

food served before a meal.
centrifugal: Outward from the center (centri- means center).
centripetal: Inward or toward the center.
multiplicity: The state of being varied and/or in large number (multi- means many). "... will crowd in on me" is a clue.
acquisitiveness: The state of acquiring or grasping things.
onslaught: Attack (-slaught refers to striking or hitting).
precepts: Principles (pre- means before; -cept- refers to taking).
solitude: Being by oneself (soli- refers to being alone).
intermittency: The state of stopping and starting again (inter- means between; -mit- means to send).

Thinking about Your Prereading Reactions

Think about how you answered the question "If you could wish for anything, what would it be?" (see page 122). How do you think Anne Morrow Lindbergh would have answered this question? How similar do you think her answer would be to yours?

Understanding Intended Meaning

Discuss the following questions with your class.

1. Describe the "shape" of Anne Morrow Lindbergh's life at home. What are some of her obligations and activities?
2. Like the crab shedding its shell, what things does the author shed while on this vacation? Make a list.
3. Describe the author's vacation house. How is it beautiful?
4. Describe the author's relationship with her sister. In what ways is it a good relationship?
5. How does the author's attitude toward physical work change now that she is at the beach?
6. While the author is on the island, how is her life different socially?
7. What is she determined to do when she returns to her life at home?

Now read the story again before proceeding to the following activities. This time you may want to examine more carefully any details you did not fully understand during your first reading.

Making Inferences

Discuss the following questions with your class.

1. The author feels that "the most exhausting thing in life . . . is being insincere" (page 124). Do you agree? What does being insincere have to do with "wearing a mask" (page 124)?
2. When describing her relationship with her sister, the author states, "The light shed by any good relationship illuminates all relationships" (page 125). What does she mean?

3. How are the author and her sister able to "[soak] up the outer world" (page 126)? Are we all capable of doing this? Explain.

4. When discussing her social life, the author reports, " . . . thrown together on this island of living, we stretch to understand each other and are invigorated by the stretching" (page 127). What is she saying? What often happens when we try to make friends with people who are very different from ourselves?

Drawing Comparisons

What is the author's attitude toward being with nature and its natural rhythms? How is this attitude comparable to the attitude Thomas Whitecloud expresses toward nature in Unit 2? Discuss your ideas with your class.

Comparing Cultural Expectations

Discuss the following questions with a small group.

1. The author says that "the life [she has] chosen as wife and mother entrains a whole caravan of complications" (see page 124). How do you think she is defining her role as wife and mother? Do you agree or disagree with her definition? Would such a definition be acceptable in the culture you know best? What about in another culture with which you are familiar? Explain.

2. The author expresses the fear that "the multiplicity of the world will crowd in on me again with its false sense of values. Values weighed in quantity, not quality; in speed, not stillness; in noise, not silence; in words, not in thoughts; in acquisitiveness, not beauty" (page 127). What does she mean? Is her fear justified? Are there cultures to which she could go where such fears would not be justified? Explain.

Relating to Self

Discuss two or more of the following questions with a partner.

1. How would you describe the "shape" of your own life? Include your own obligations and activities.

2. What are a few of the simple pleasures important to your life? Describe them.

3. Like Anne Morrow Lindbergh, have you ever been so involved in your work that you forgot yourself, the people you were with, and what you were going to do next? What was the situation? How did being so involved in your work make you feel? What event brought you back to your obligations and daily activities?

4. What did you like best about the author's relationship with her sister? Describe a similar relationship you have had. What advantages do such relationships have?

Appreciating Descriptive Language

Discuss the following ideas with your class and your teacher.

1. You learned in Unit 4 that descriptive language often involves a comparison between two things that are not usually thought to be alike. An example from *Gift from the Sea* would be Anne Morrow Lindbergh's comparing the tracks left behind by the hermit crab to "a delicate vine on the sand" (page 123). This is an unusual but very vivid comparison. Look at the following comparisons. Decide what two things are being compared in each case, and write them, one on each side of the equal symbol (=). See the example.

Example: "Its shape [referring to the shell], swelling like a pear in the center . . . " (page 123).

The shell's shape = The pear's shape.

a. "Island living has been a lens through which to examine my own life in the North" (page 127).

_____ = _____

b. "I shall turn it [the week she has spent with her sister] around like a shell, testing and analyzing its good points" (page 125).

_____ = _____

c. " . . . the sandpipers ahead of us move like a corps of ballet dancers keeping time to some interior rhythm inaudible to us" (page 126).

_____ = _____

Sometimes a comparison becomes more complex and a relationship is drawn, as in the following example:

. . . they [the cobwebs] soften the hard lines of the rafters as grey hairs soften the lines on a middle-aged face (page 125).

Here, the relationship itself is being compared. Complete the comparison.

_____Cobwebs_____ are to _____rafters_____ as

_____ are to _____ .

With your class and the teacher, discuss any other comparisons that you feel are important to the meaning of Gift from the Sea.

2. The shell becomes many things to the author. For example, it becomes a house when she states, "I shall ask into my shell only those friends with whom I can be completely honest" (page 124). What other things do shells become in this selection?

3. What do you think is meant by the title Gift from the Sea? Do you see any symbolism in its words? (Refer back to Unit 7, page 92 for a discussion of symbolism.) Do you feel the title is appropriate for the author's book?

Others, too, have found joy in simplicity. The author of the following poem expresses the idea that one doesn't need to travel far to experience such pleasure.

I Have Found Such Joy

Grace Noll Crowell

I have found such joy in simple things;
    A plain, clean room, a nut-brown loaf of bread,
A cup of milk, a kettle as it sings,
    The shelter of a roof above my head,
And in a leaf-laced square along the floor,
Where yellow sunlight glimmers through a door.

I have found such joy in things that fill
    My quiet days: a curtain's blowing grace,
A potted plant upon my window sill,
    A rose, fresh-cut and placed within a vase;
A table cleared, a lamp beside a chair,
And books I long have loved beside me there.

Oh, I have found such joys I wish I might
    Tell every woman who goes seeking far
For some elusive, feverish delight,
    That very close to home the great joys are:
The elemental things—old as the race,
Yet never, through the ages, commonplace.

elusive: *Not easily obtained.*
elemental: *Basic.*

Understanding Intended Meaning

Discuss the following questions with your class.

1. What kinds of things bring joy to the poet? List a few.

2. What advice does the poet give women? Do you think the same advice would also be good for men? Explain.

Relating to Self

Make a list of the things that bring joy into your life. You may want to write a simple poem using "I Have Found Such Joy" as a guide. Share your list or your poem with a partner.

Developing Your Word Bank

List in your Word Bank (see page 152) a few of the words or phrases from this unit that are new to you. Choose only those items that you feel will be useful. You may want to work with a partner or have your teacher help you with this task. Consider words you might want to use in conversation, in writing, or in communication about an academic area in which you have a special interest.

Ideas for Discussion and/or Writing

Choose one or more of the following activities.

1. Begin a journal in which you make entries two or three times a week. Perhaps you are already keeping a journal (see page 17). Include in the entries your thoughts about the complications in your own life and how you deal with them on a daily basis. Include also some of the simple pleasures you experience. You may want to share your journal with your teacher and/or another student from time to time.

2. What are your own ideas about freedom from the complications of life? Does freedom mean not meeting obligations? Describe in detail your views. Give examples where appropriate.

3. Create a short scenario in which two or more of the following people are having a conversation: Thomas Whitecloud (from Unit 2), Richard Cory (from Unit 4), Kino and Juana (from Unit 4), and Anne Morrow Lindbergh (from this unit). In the conversation, have the people discuss, among other things, what they think happiness is. Have them relate their comments to their own lives. You may want to have class members volunteer to act out the scenario.

4. With a group of three to six students, organize a television talk show. Have one person play the role of the talk show host and the others play the roles of people interviewed. Select from the following list those individuals you want interviewed: Thomas Whitecloud, Richard Cory, Kino, Juana, and Anne Morrow Lindbergh. Beforehand, create a list of possible questions that the host might ask each person.

5. Anne Morrow Lindbergh describes the beach as a favorite place that brings her both joy and peace. Describe your favorite place. In what ways is it like the beach the author describes?

Notes

1. Refers to the sixteenth- and seventeenth-century Protestants who came to America from England.
2. Martha was a friend of Jesus in the Bible. She was often concerned with cleaning, cooking, and other household duties.
3. A German word meaning the state of being disunited or strife-torn.

10

IMAGES OF GROWING OLD

As people grow old, some fear changes in physical appearance such as thinning hair and deepening wrinkles. Others are more concerned with the possibility of losing both physical and mental health. In spite of these fears, there are many who maintain a positive outlook toward growing old. They see it as a time to enjoy themselves and take pride in lives well lived. Some, too, find greater self-acceptance and increased wisdom. Discuss your own attitudes toward old age with a partner.

Fond memories and loving relationships can often ease the suffering of old age. With a partner, read the following poem about an elderly couple who, in spite of being old, continue to bring joy and richness into each other's lives. You and your partner may want to take turns reading the stanzas aloud. Together try to discover the poem's meaning.

The First Snow of the Year

Mark Van Doren

The old man, listening to the careful
Steps of his old wife as up she came,
Up, up, so slowly, then her slippered
Progress down the long hall to their door—

Outside the wind, wilder suddenly,
Whirled the first snow of the year; danced
Round and round with it, coming closer
And closer, peppering the panes; now here she was—

Said "Ah, my dear, remember?" But his tray
Took all of her attention, having to hold it
Level. "Ah, my dear, don't you remember?"
"What?" "That time we walked in the white woods."

She handed him his napkin; felt the glass
To make sure the milk in it was warm;
Sat down; got up again; brought comb and brush
To tidy his top hair. "Yes, I remember."

He wondered if she saw now what he did.
Possibly not. An afternoon so windless,
The huge flakes rustled upon each other,
Filling the woods, the world, with cold, cold—

---

slippered progress: Wearing slippers and progressing or moving forward.

peppering: Sprinkling as though with pepper.
rustled: Made whispering sounds caused by surfaces coming together.
" . . . upon each other" is a clue.

They shivered, having a long way to go,
And then their mittens touched; and touched again;
Their eyes, trying not to meet, did meet;
They stopped, and in the cold held out their arms

Till she came into his; awkwardly,
As girl to boy that never kissed before,
The woods, the darkening world, so cold, so cold,
While these two burned together. He remembered,

And wondered if she did, how like a sting,
A hidden heat it was; while there they stood
And trembled, and the snow made statues of them.
"Ah, my dear, remember?" "Yes, I do."

She rocked and thought: he wants me to say something.
But we said nothing then. The main thing is,
I'm with him still; he calls me and I come.
But slowly. Time makes sluggards of us all.

"Yes, I do remember." The wild wind
Was louder, but a sweetness in her speaking
Stung him, and he heard. While round and round
The first snow of the year danced on the lawn.

sluggards: Slow-moving persons. "But slowly" is a clue.

Understanding Intended Meaning

Discuss the following questions with your class.

1. Describe the situation in which we find the old man and his wife. Who is taking care of whom? Why? Where are they? What is happening outside?

2. Tell about the experience they remember from the past.

3. How would you describe their relationship? Is it supportive? Is it happy? How do you know?

Identifying Point of View

From whose point of view is the poem told? Does the point of view shift? Discuss your answers with your class and the teacher. You may want to review the discussion of point of view in Unit 3 on page 42.

Appreciating Descriptive Language

Discuss the following questions with your class and the teacher.

1. In Unit 4 you learned that descriptive language often involves a comparison between two things that are not usually thought to be alike. In addition, you learned in Unit 2 that a comparison in which an object or idea is given human qualities is called personification. Explain the comparisons used in the following lines. Do you see personification in any of them?

Lines in which Descriptive Language Is Found	**Explanation**
"Outside the wind, wilder suddenly, Whirled the first snow of the year; danced Round and round with it . . . " (page 137).	
" . . . how like a sting, A hidden heat it was . . . " (page 138).	
" . . . the snow made statues of them" (page 138).	

2. Does the use of the descriptive language above increase your enjoyment of the poem? Explain.

In the following personal essay, Elizabeth Yates wrestles with the subject of growing old and uncovers many of its positive aspects. Based on her own experience, she reveals a keen insight into the importance of pursuing one's work and remaining active far into old age. Through her, we see a triumph of the spirit over what to many may seem a time of overwhelming sadness and despair.

from **Always Ahead**

Elizabeth Yates

At six she had been told she was a big girl now. She was excited about going to school. She clutched hard the hand of the grown-up that held hers as they went up the steps of the big building, through the door, and to the entrance of the classroom; then she had to let go, had to face that room full of children, some few she knew but many she had never seen before.

As the tall teacher came toward her, she felt her hand slip from the familiar grasp and suddenly she was alone—only herself and that new experience. She couldn't turn around and run away. She couldn't cry out to the grown-up retreating. She could only go forward and in that moment of time she felt something take hold of her inside—a new something. It was courage. She said "Good morning" to the teacher as she had been told to do, said her name, then went toward the desk that had been pointed out as hers. Yes, she was a big girl now, ready to face what was ahead.

Elizabeth Yates, a writer of children's books, is known internationally. She was born in 1905 in Buffalo, New York. Having spent much of her own childhood on a farm, she learned the value of focusing on the positive aspects of life. This focus comes through in much of her writing.

clutched: *Grasped.*
retreating: *Going back or withdrawing (re- here means back).*

Time went by and it was her tenth birthday that was being celebrated. Even bigger was the day when she entered the teens. There were other great occasions. To be sixteen was one, and then to be twenty-one: a grown-up who could vote, a young woman who could take her own stand. Each stage of growing had blended into the next effortlessly, inevitably. Yes, always there would be something ahead. This was the learning that was life; and the savor, too.

From a vantage point of years I look back on her now: how eager she had been to do the work that she knew was hers to do, the work with words; how blest she had been to find one with whom she would share the greater part of her life through marriage with its delights and disciplines. As they grew to know each other, they found out more about themselves and felt at home in life. It was not always easy, but sorrow was balanced by joy and hard times were offset by gains in understanding. Everything could be shared: books, travel, experiences, ideas, spiritual discoveries, and long, long talks about God.

They had climbed mountains, run rivers, slept under the stars by campfires, visited sophisticated cities, and stayed in small villages. Pictures had been taken so the times could be relived, and small treasures purchased that would remind them of places visited. It had all been good, even the hard times.

It was difficult to tell herself that "the best is yet to be" when the time came that she was alone. He had died, that was all, and it was up to her now to find her own way. Alone but not lonely: that was the pact she made with herself. She was realistic enough to know that there would be deserts to cross and mountains to climb. She would accept the challenge as on that first day in school when she had found what was needed to face the unknown. Courage.

The facts said she was old. Old was a beautiful word; but so misunderstood, so maligned. A house that was weathered and sheltered for centuries was honored; wine that had mellowed for years was respected; antiques had high prices placed on them; and there were few who could buy themselves an old car, so costly was it. People in fulfilling their years became antiques. Appraisals of their value might vary, but they deserved honor and respect. She had some friends, a few years ahead of her, whom she held dear for their calm, their wisdom. They carried their years well like a packsack full of surprises. Though infirmity might have compelled them to live with limited activity, nothing had happened to their minds, their hearts.

There were others to whom time was an enemy to be fought, though secretly they knew the battle was a losing one. "I don't like what's happening to me!" "I don't want to be old." Such useless notions. Yield was the word now, yield to the rhythm of life. It was vitality that mattered. "How young you look" was a foolish comment, as if youth were the norm. "How well you look" was a tonic.

She felt no different in her inmost self, but outwardly there were changes. There was a lessening of energy so that things took longer to do. There was a tendency to withdraw, but of this she knew she must be watchful. However limited life might become, it was essential to keep in stride though the pace might be slower.

---

teens: *Ages thirteen through nineteen.*
inevitably: *Without the possibility of being avoided.*
savor: *Here it means something that adds zest or excitement.*
vantage point: *A position giving advantage.*
pact: *An agreement.*
maligned: *(pronounced "mə-līn'-d") Defamed or slandered (mal- means bad). ". . . so misunderstood" is a clue.*
mellowed: *Become full-flavored and rich tasting; not harsh or bitter.*
antiques: *Things made during an earlier period of time (anti-*

here means before). The other items in the list (e.g., old car) are clues.
appraisals: *Determinations of how much something is worth.*
infirmity: *Illness or weakness (in- here means not; -firm- means strong).*
yield: *Give in or surrender.*
vitality: *Liveliness or energy (vita- means life).*
norm: *The thing that is standard or the average.*
tonic: *Something that gives vitality.*

Her group of friends began to decrease. Some went to the comfort of retirement homes, some to the unknown. There were stalwart ones who still enjoyed travel and chided her because she now chose to stay at home. Through books and in her imagination she did travel. There were many places she had never been—up the longest river to its source or the highest mountain to its summit. She had not been where past civilizations had lived and disappeared, or gone below the ocean to discover what undersea life was like.

Travel now required neither passport nor travelers' checks, and the itinerary she laid out herself. No new clothes were needed except as worn ones were replaced. No phrase books, no luggage. It would be all right, she persuaded herself, if she went into it with the enthusiasm and curiosity she had had for distant lands. So she began to make herself ready. She cut down on commitments and schooled herself to say no to many things she had done because she felt she should and settled on things she really wanted to do. Time that had once seemed so pressured was now available. There were others moving forward in the progression of life who would take her place; they were younger with new ideas and a resource of strength. She began to find advantages that offset the relinquishments; and as her own senses became less sharp, she discovered a deepening sensitivity for others. She gave herself little treats—breakfast in bed, a cup of tea to rest her, dinner out with a friend.

Things were coming to her more and one of the first lessons she had to learn was to accept them with grace. Love was more widely shared. Disappointments hurt less. Time seemed to be providing an immunity. She grew more selective as she willingly took on change as the pattern of life. And it required courage.

Letting go of the past with its habits, its set ways of doing things, she tightened her hold on the thread that had been guiding her, and she expected the good. She would look for it and make it happen.

Now it seemed that it was not so much a journey she was making as a graduate course she was taking. She filled one notebook with her discoveries and bought another. When a new thing came her way she endeavored to move along something old—clothing, equipment, whatever was not necessary. Finish small tasks the day they were begun and give the next day its own leeway. This was all part of growing; and achievement, however slight, made her feel competent to handle the present.

Simplify. Do things the easiest way. See friends often but, whether food is involved or not, know that conversation is the real nutrient. Take nothing for granted: show your appreciation, express your gratitude, be generous with affection. The words "used to" could be a trap; better far was it to substitute "This is the way now."

A young friend said to her one day, "It must be awful to be old."

She had taken a long moment to reply. "Yes, it is awe-ful. So much is being done these days to keep people living longer, living well, that we who are old have a great responsibility to live our lives fully; to do what can be done and bring to it something of what we have learned; to show that life is still rich and good; to face reality and discover our strength."

"I see what you mean," the young one said.

But did she? Didn't one have to be old before one could talk about what it was like?

"And the best is yet to be." So softly she said

---

stalwart: Here it means not giving up physically or mentally.
". . . still enjoyed travel" is a clue.
chided: Scolded.
summit: Highest point. ". . . highest mountain" is a clue.
itinerary: The route proposed for a journey.
relinquishments: Things given up or left behind (re- here means behind; -linquish- refers to leaving).

immunity: The state of not being affected by something.
"Disappointments hurt less" is a clue.
endeavored: Tried hard.
move along something: Here it means to give something to someone else.
leeway: Greater freedom.
nutrient: That which helps something to grow and develop.
awe-ful: A made-up word meaning full of awe or wonder.

the words that they might have been inaudible.

Her wants had lessened and her needs were few, except for the continuing one of quiet. Aloneness. Hours during which she might read, or listen to music, or just be. The world around her had so much for her to absorb. The trees in their leaf-leaving were glorious, not only in their color but in the ballet made by the leaves as they found their way to the ground. Always this beauty had been, but she felt more sensitive to it than ever. There was a day, sitting in her garden, when distantly she heard the sound of geese in their migration. Looking at the sky she saw them, just visible in the morning mist— a perfect V; yet even as she watched, the leader fell back into the formation and another moved forward to take that place. This would go on and on, long after she could follow their flight across the sky: always one ready to draw back so another could come forward. These were not unusual happenings, but they gave her much to think about, to weave into her own life and where she was in time.

Always there was something ahead, perhaps only a small event like a concert or a friend coming to see her. Looking forward gave incentive to her days. Life had had great moments; looking back she could recall many of them as she thought her way through the decades.

I know her well, that little girl growing through life's stages from childhood to old age, each one preparing her for the next. I can remember her feeling when on that first day of school she let go of the hand that held hers, the feeling that came from within and that sent her forward, and with it, uncertainty and trepidation had dissolved.

---

inaudible: *Incapable of being heard (-aud- refers to hearing). "So softly she said the words" is a clue.*
migration: *Here it means a seasonal move to another region (migrate means to move).*

incentive: *Something causing one to be active or to put forth effort.*
trepidation: *A state of fearfulness.*
dissolved: *Here it means disappeared (dis- means apart; -solve- means to loosen).*

Thinking about Your Prereading Reactions

Return to page 136, where you were asked to discuss your own attitudes toward old age. How close do your attitudes come to those expressed by Elizabeth Yates in the selection you just read?

Understanding Intended Meaning

Discuss the following questions with your class.

1. Describe how the author felt at the age of six when she first went to school. In what ways was that experience similar to other experiences in her life now that she is old? What one word names the "something within" that she would always call upon in times of need? Why is this word appropriate?

2. How does the author describe her marriage?

3. The author claims that old is "a beautiful word" (page 142). According to her, what things improve with age? How might people be like these things?

4. What is the author's attitude toward travel now that she is old? How does she prefer to "travel" now? In what other ways is her life changing? Include both negative and positive elements.

5. How is the title of this selection appropriate?

Making Inferences

Discuss the following questions with your class.

1. What is the difference between saying "How *young* you look" and "How *well* you look"? (See page 142.) Which one is a foolish comment according to the author? Explain.

2. The author reports that a young friend said to her, "It must be awful to be old." Her response was, "Yes, it is awe-ful." (See page 143.) What does she mean by this play on words?

3. React to the author's argument that "however limited life might become, it [is] essential to keep in stride though the pace might be slower" (page 142). What does she mean by this statement? Do you agree?

4. In what way was time "providing an immunity" to her life as an elderly person (page 143)?

Drawing Comparisons

Do you see any similarities between the author's ideas as expressed in this essay and those of Anne Morrow Lindbergh in Unit 9? Consider their attitudes toward life and its joys and commitments. What other persons (authors or characters) included in this book seem to share attitudes similar to these? Discuss your ideas with a small group.

Relating to Self

Discuss the following questions with a partner.

1. What does it mean to be "alone but not lonely" (page 142)? Have you ever felt this way? Explain.

2. The author reports giving herself "little treats" in her old age (for example, "dinner out with a friend"). (See page 143.) When you become old, what "little treats" might you more frequently give yourself?

Comparing Cultural Expectations

In some cultures, talk about old age and death is generally avoided in casual conversation. These cultures are sometimes referred to as "death-defying cultures" because they do not readily acknowledge death as one of life's natural occurrences. It is as though death, if ignored, will somehow go away. Even the dying people themselves are sometimes shunned by persons whose fear keeps them at a distance. How is death handled in the culture you know best? How are dying people treated? Do you notice differences in cultural attitudes toward old age and death? Discuss your ideas with a small group.

Appreciating Descriptive Language

In Unit 7 you learned that symbolism is a type of descriptive language. You learned that a symbol is an idea or concept used to represent another idea or concept. Sometimes the symbolism can become very complex, especially when it involves whole actions or situations. For example, children playing with toy guns and setting up rules for each other might represent adults at war. Or vines growing wildly in tangled masses over smooth rocks might represent the problems that we allow to clutter our lives. The symbolism intended by an author can be quite clear although not directly stated. What symbolism might be present in the following description by Elizabeth Yates?

Looking at the sky she saw them, just visible in the morning mist—a perfect V; yet even as she watched, the leader fell back into the formation and another moved forward to take that place. This would go on and on, long after she could follow their flight across the sky: always one ready to draw back so another could come forward (page 144).

What do the geese represent? Explain what the actions of falling back and moving forward in formation might mean. What clues led you to your conclusions? Did you notice any other examples of symbolism in this essay? Discuss your ideas with members of your class and the teacher.

Reading Critically

Discuss the following questions with your class.

Some descriptive language may involve expressions you have heard over and over again, such as *blue as the sky,* or *the autumn of life* (meaning old age). We say that such overused expressions are *trite.* Did any of the descriptive language used in this essay strike you as being trite? For example, consider the following passage:

She was realistic enough to know that there would be deserts to cross and mountains to climb. She would accept the challenge as on that first day in school . . . (page 142).

What do the deserts and mountains symbolize? Have you heard these words used in similar expressions before? Do they in any way seem trite to you? Are there any other examples in this essay of what you might consider to be trite descriptive language?

Identifying Point of View

The author writes this essay using the third person *she.* Does this in any way seem unnatural to you? Why do you think she uses the third person? Do you think the essay would have been better had she referred to herself as *I*? Explain.

The following poem was thought to have been written in 1692 by an unknown author. According to a widely spread rumor, it was found on the door of Old Saint Paul's Church in Baltimore, Maryland. In reality, it was written in 1927 by an Indiana poet named Max Ehrmann. Its words have been very meaningful to people of many different cultures and religions. It speaks not so much about the elderly and the nearness of death (although it addresses these topics too), but about life and how to make it full and rich even into old age. The title, "Desiderata," is a Latin word meaning things that are desired (in this case, things that are desired in life).

from **Desiderata**
Max Ehrmann

Go placidly amid the noise and haste,

and remember what peace there may be in silence.

As far as possible without surrender

be on good terms with all persons.

Speak your truth quietly and clearly,

even to the dull and ignorant.

They too have their story.

Avoid loud and aggressive persons,

they are vexatious to the spirit.

If you compare yourself with others,

you may become vain or bitter; for always

there will be greater and lesser persons than yourself.

Enjoy your achievements as well as your plans.

Keep interested in your career, however humble;

it is a real possession in the changing fortunes of time.

Exercise caution in your business affairs;

for the world is full of trickery.

But let this not blind you to what virtue there is;

many persons strive for high ideals;

and everywhere life is full of heroism.

Be yourself. Especially do not feign affection.

---

placidly: *Calmly (plac- refers to pleasing). ". . . Remember what peace there may be" is a clue.*
amid: *An old-fashioned word meaning among (mid means middle).*

vexatious: *(pronounced "vĕk-sā'-shəs") Annoying or disturbing.*
feign: *Pretend.*

Neither be cynical about love; for in the face of all

disenchantment it is perennial as the grass.

Take kindly the counsel of the years,

gracefully surrendering the things of youth.

Nurture strength of spirit to shield you in sudden misfortune.

But do not distress yourself with dark imaginings.

Many fears are born of fatigue and loneliness.

Beyond a wholesome discipline, be gentle with yourself.

You are a child of the universe,

no less than the trees and the stars.

You have a right to be here.

And whether or not it is clear to you,

no doubt the universe is unfolding as it should.

. . . . . .

Keep peace in your soul.

With all its shame, drudgery and broken dreams,

it is still a beautiful world.

Be cheerful. Strive to be happy.

---

cynical: *Full of scorn.*
disenchantment: *Here it means loss of wonder or enchantment (dis- means not).*
perennial: *Appearing over and over again (per- means throughout; -enni- refers to year). "... as the grass" is a clue.*

counsel: *Advice.*
nurture: *Here it means encourage or promote the development of (nurt- refers to feeding).*
wholesome: *Healthy.*
drudgery: *Extremely unpleasant work.*

Understanding Intended Meaning

In your own words, write what advice you think the poem you just read is giving about the following general topics:

silence: _____

_____

socializing: _____

_____

jealousy: _____

_____

goals: _____

_____

work/career: _____

_____

business: _____

_____

love: _____

_____

old age: _____

_____

fear: _____

_____

Compare your interpretations with those of a partner. Make any changes you wish based on what you learn.

Reading Critically

Do you agree with the advice given about each topic above? What might you change? Would you add anything? Discuss your ideas with a small group.

Developing Your Word Bank

List in your Word Bank (see page 152) a few of the words or phrases from this unit that are new to you. Choose only those items that you feel will be useful. You may want to work with a partner or have your teacher help you with this task. Consider words you might want to use in conversation, in writing, or in communication about an academic area in which you have a special interest.

Ideas for Discussion and/or Writing

Choose one or more of the following activities.

1. Imagine that you are very old. Describe a day in your life. Tell about your activities, foods, shelter, clothing, friends, and anything else you feel may be important. Think too about changes that may have taken place not only in yourself but in the world around you. You may want to include some of these changes in your description.

2. Compare the attitudes toward growing old of two cultures with which you are familiar. Consider both negative and positive aspects. Can you explain any of the differences that you have observed?

3. Write your own "Desiderata." Include all of the things that you think are important to leading a full and rich life. Share your paper with a partner. Ask your partner to write a brief response, including areas of agreement or disagreement. You may want to react in writing to your partner's response, thus continuing the dialogue.

4. Think about someone you admire who is very old. Tell about that person's life and why you hold that person in such high esteem.

5. Choose one of the topics from "Desiderata," such as silence, love, old age, or fear. Write your own personal essay about the topic. Use several examples to support your point of view. You might also want to refer to what others have said about the subject. Check with your school librarian and/or teacher for possible sources.

WORD BANK

Make your list of useful words and phrases in this section of the book. After each word or phrase you list, briefly write its meaning. If you use a dictionary, choose the definition that you think comes closest to the way the item is used in the reading selection. You may want to note other useful meanings as well. Then use the word or phrase in an appropriate context (you can take the context directly from the selection in which you found the item). You may want to work with a partner or have your teacher help you with this task. Your teacher or a partner may quiz you on the words or phrases from time to time. See the sample entry below.

Sample Entry

Selection: "Blue Winds Dancing"

Words and Phrases:

1. silhouetted = (pronounced "sĭl-oo-ĕt'-ĭd") Appearing to be outlined and filled in with black.

    context: "A deer comes out of the woods just ahead of me and stands _silhouetted_ on the rails" (p. 20).

2. velvet vests = Sleeveless tops that button down the front and are made of a very soft cloth with a raised surface similar to fur.

    context: The men wore velvet vests.

selection: "Blue Winds Dancing"

+ crunches : (krʌnt) to chew with a noisy, grinding sound make a crushing sound.

- Sprawled : (sprôl) to sit or lie with the limbs spread out awkwardly.

- etched : (ech) : formed as though their outlines have been into the sky.

- intellectual : (adj) (ĭn'tĭĕk chŏŏ·al) : of the intellect having or showing superior reasoning power.

+ moccasin : (mŏk'a-sĭn) n : A soft leather slipper or shoe.

"THE RED DOG"

+ customary : (adj) (kŭs'ta-mĕr, ē) commonly practiced or used ; usual.

- blurt (v) (blûrt) to say suddenly and impulsively. say quickly without thought.

- padding (pădíng) n : Material that is used to pad working with soft steps.

- choked out (chŏk) ready to cry. to terminate ; interfere with.

+ astounded (a-stound')v. to strike with confusion and wonder amazed

PEALS

+ utterly : (adv. ut'ər-lē) completely, absolutely; entirely.

- petulant : (adj) (pech'ŏŏ-lent) unreasonably irritable or ill-tempered; peevish.

- cleft : (v kleft) A split or division between two parts

- erosion : (n ĭ-rō'zhən) the action or result of wearing away by nature.

+ scurried : (v skûr'e) to scamper, to rush move quickly with light, short steps.

THE GREAT HOUDIN.

+ suicide : (n sŏŏ'ĭ-sīd) The act or an instance of intentionally killing oneself.
        - one who commits.

- porpoise : (n, pôr'pəs) A marine mammal related to the whales but smaller, usually having a blunt snout and triangular dorsal fin.

+ ingenuity (n, in'jə-nŏŏ'ĭ-tenyə') inventive skill or imagination; cleverness.

- conjuring (v, kŏn'jər, kənjŏŏr') using magic to cause something to appear.

- unveiled : (v ŭn-vāl') to remove a veil from
        - to disclose reveal.

        Here it mean demonstrated openly to be viewed by all

compensations

brazenly :

admonition :

precisely

husky .

Final.

Adjective clauses.

Vocab - Concepts for today.

Review all articles since midterm

Exploring themes "Cecilia Rosas" "The Rose"

One new words chapter 7-12 except 10

chapter 8.

- what news from defy (example)

- page 224

GLOSSARY

Several of the words included in this glossary have more than one meaning. The meanings given here are generally consistent with the way the words are used in this book.

absorption: The state of being pulled into something completely.

accustomed: Customary.

acquisitiveness: The state of acquiring or grasping things.

acrobatics: Performance demonstrating skill in moving the body in various positions. Often balance is involved.

acute: Here it means sharp (*acu-* refers to a needle or point).

administrator: One who is in charge (*ad-* here means to; *-minist-* refers to serving).

admonitions: Warnings or advice.

afield: Away.

agitation: Disturbance.

algae: A group of sea plants, including seaweed.

alight: An old-fashioned way of saying lit up.

allegiance: Loyalty.

amid: An old-fashioned word meaning among (*mid* means middle).

amulet: A charm against evil.

anesthetic: A substance that makes one less sensitive to pain.

antiques: Things made during an earlier period of time (*anti-* here means before).

apathetically: Without emotion or interest (*a-* here means without; *-pathe-* refers to feeling).

apex: The highest point or the top.

apparent: Obvious or visible (*appar-* refers to appearing).

appeasingly: In an attempt to bring peace or to soothe.

appraisals: Determinations of how much something is worth.

apprehension: Dread or fear.

apprehensively: Fearfully; uneasily.

architecture: The basic design of a structure.

arrogance: The state of being filled with self-importance.

arthritis: A painful swelling in the joints of the body.

articulation: Here it means the act of speaking.

aspens: Fast-growing whitish colored trees with shiny leaves.

asserted: Came forward boldly.

astounded: Amazed.

avalanche: A large mass of falling snow.

awe-ful: A made-up word meaning full of awe or wonder.

barnacles: Small, hard-shelled sea animals that attach themselves to surfaces under water.

bask: Enjoy the warmth.

beaded: Covered with beads.

beckoned: Invited someone or something to come using a nod or a gesture.

benign: Harmless (*beni-* refers to well).

bewildered: Puzzled.

birch bark: The pale or white outer covering of a birch tree.

biscuits: Small cakes of bread made without yeast.

bitch: A female dog or similar animal.

blast: Here it means the loud blowing of a horn.

blazing: Extremely and intensely hot (*blaze* means to burn like a hot flame).

bleak: Depressing.

blizzard: A severe snowstorm.

blotted out: Gotten rid of; destroyed.

blurted out: Said quickly without thought.

boughs: Large branches of a tree.

bound to: Here it means very likely to.

bourgeois: (pronounced "boor-zhwä") The middle class.

braced: Supported or held upright.

brazenly: Boldly.

breeds: Gives birth to.

bristle: Cause one's hair to stand up or become erect.

brutally: Painfully (a *brute* is an animal without feeling).

burgeoned: Grew rapidly.

bustle about: Hurry around in an excited state.

capsized: Overturned.

caravan: Usually a group of vehicles, people, or animals moving one behind the other.

carcass: A dead body.

caresses: Gentle touches.

casuarina: Trees having small scalelike leaves.

centrifugal: Outward from the center (*centri-* means center).

centripetal: Inward or toward the center.

chastely: Purely or innocently.

chauvinistic: Believing that one's own group is superior to others.

cherished: Held dear or treasured.

chidden: Scolded. *Chided* is a more widely used word meaning the same thing.

chided: Scolded.

choked up: Ready to cry.

cicadas: Flying insects that make a dull humming sound.

circulation: Here it means the movement of blood around the body (*cir-* means around or circle).

circumference: Here it means the boundary line of an area (*circum-* means around).

civilian: Relating to ordinary citizens, those not in the armed forces (*civi-* refers to citizen).

clambered: Climbed with difficulty.

clawing: Scratching or digging into a surface as if with claws.

cleft: A split or division between two parts.

clutched: Grasped.

cluttered: Filled with things in an unorganized way.

cocked: Tilted or turned up. Also means to put the hammer of a gun in position for firing.

coiled: Arranged in a circle.

collapsed: Fell into ruin or broke down.

color barrier: Obstacles because of one's race.

commitment: Here it means the acceptance of certain responsibilities regarding another person.

compelling: Irresistible or forceful (*com-* means together; *-pel-* means drive or force).

compensations: Things received which are equal to or which make up for things lost.

complacency: Self-satisfaction.

conception: Here it means idea or concept.

confinement: The state of being shut into an enclosure.

conflagration: A large fire.

conjuring: Using magic to cause something to appear.

conscience: One's sense of right and wrong (*con-* refers to with; *-science* refers to knowing).

consequences: The results that naturally follow an action or condition (*con-* means with; *-seque-* means to follow).

conserve: Save or keep from being lost.

contain: Here it means to hold something inside (*con-* means together; *-tain* refers to holding).

contentment: The state of being satisfied or content.

contortionist: A person who can twist his or her body and limbs into unusual positions (*con-* means together; *-tort-* refers to twisting).

contrived: Invented.

corps: (pronounced "kor") A group of individuals moving together in one direction.

counsel: Advice.

country-bred: Raised in the country.

cramped: Crowded.

creaks: Makes a squeaking sound.

creek trail: The trail formed by a frozen creek.

crevice: A narrow opening or crack (*crev-* refers to a crack or split).

critical: Here it means serious and important.

crouched: Bent down with limbs close to the body.

cruises: Travels.

crumpled up: Collapsed.

crunches: Makes a crushing sound.

cunning: Sly.

curious: Here it means odd or unexpected.

cursed: Declared to be evil; swore or used profane language.

customary: Usual.

cynical: Full of scorn.

cynically: Scornfully or bitterly.

cypress: An evergreen tree with very small needles. It grows in warm climates.

daily grind: The day-to-day routine.

dashing: Dressed in the latest fashions. This word is seldom used today.

daubed: Applied with quick strokes.

daze: The state of having dulled senses.

dazed: Stunned and overwhelmed.

deceit: Falseness.

defenses: Things used to defend or protect.

delusions: False beliefs.

derisively: In a manner that makes fun of someone or something.

despair: To lose all hope.

devised: Planned or invented.

dignity: Self-respect.

dimension: Here it means size.

diplomas: Official papers stating the specific degree title completed.

disenchantment: Here it means loss of wonder or enchantment (*dis-* means not).

dissolved: Here it means disappeared.

distinctly: In a well-defined way (*distin-* refers to separating).

distorted: Twisted (*-tort-* means to twist).

domestic: Referring to the home or household (*domes-* means house).

dominated: Controlled (*domina-* refers to a lord or master).

doused: Wet thoroughly.

down in the dumps: Depressed.

drenched: Soaked all the way through.

drifts: Flows gently.

drudgery: Extremely unpleasant work.
elemental: Basic.
elusive: Not easily obtained.
emerged: Came up out of.
encumbrance: A burden.
endeavored: Tried hard.
endured: Continued to bear.
ensued: Followed (*en-* here means onward).
entanglement: The state of being twisted together.
entertained: Here it means held in one's mind to think about carefully (*enter–* means between; *–tain–* refers to holding).
entrains: Pulls along (*-train-* refers to pulling or drawing along).
epically heroic feats: Great deeds that are similar to what heroes might accomplish in epics (long poems that tell stories).
erosion: The action or result of wearing away by nature .
essence: The most important element that gives something its identity.
etched: Formed as though their outlines have been cut into the sky with a sharp instrument.
excruciating: Extremely painful.
executives: Persons running a company or organization.
exhibition: A show or display for the public (*ex-* means out; *-hibi-* refers to holding).
exotic: Unfamiliar and exciting (*ex-* means outside).
exploits: Heroic acts.
expose: Here it means reveal or unmask.
extending: Here it means spreading out (*ex-* means out; *-tend-* refers to stretching).
extremities: The parts of the body that are farthest from the center; usually refers to the hands and feet (*ex-* means out).
facades: False fronts (*faca-* refers to face.)
face the actuality: Accept as fact.
fall through the cracks: Are ignored.
feign: Pretend.
feline: Like a cat.
fern-like: Like a fern, a flowerless green plant.
fetched forth: Brought forward or into view.
flagged: Made of flagstone, which is a flat stone split into pieces and used to make a cover over the ground.
flared: Burned or shone brightly for a short time.
flotsam: Here it means pieces of wood drifting together.
floundered: Moved clumsily to try to regain one's footing.
flung: Threw violently or with force (the past tense of fling).
folly: Foolishness.
footgear: Clothing worn on the feet.
forbidding: Unfriendly or grim.
forefeet: Front feet (*fore-* means front).
fork: Here it means one of the streams into which a creek is divided.
foster: Aid in the development of.
fraudulent: Dishonest or extremely misleading (*fraud* means trickery).
frivolous: Silly or lighthearted.
fully freighted: Carrying as much as it could hold; loaded (*freight* usually refers to goods carried commercially).
gadgets: Small mechanical devices used for specific purposes.
galleries: Buildings in which artwork is displayed for public view.

game: The animals that are killed by hunters.
gaping: Staring in wonder with one's mouth open.
gazed: Stared. **geraniums:** A type of plant with brightly colored flowers and divided leaves.
germane: Related to or consistent with.
gesticulate: Gesture.
gibbered: Spoke nonsense.
glimmerings: Indications (*glim-* means a source of light).
glint: A flash of light or sparkle.
glorious: Deserving glory or highest praise.
grimaced: Showed disgust by twisting the face out of shape.
groan: Make a moaning sound.
grudge: A deep-seated resentment.
gruff: Harsh.
gushed: Forced out in a sudden burst.
hailed: Greeted.
hale and hearty: An old-fashioned way to say healthy.
harmony: Together in a pleasing way (*harmon-* refers to joining).
heady: Here it means capable of overwhelming the senses.
hearing-impaired: People who have difficulty hearing (to *impair* means to reduce strength or ability).
heaved: Here it means pushed or moved up with great effort.
hemispheres: Here it means the eastern and western halves of the world (*hemi-* means half; *-sphere-* means ball or globe).
hermit crab: A soft-bodied crab that lives in and carries the empty shell of another animal.
hired hands: People who are paid for work that they usually do with their hands.
hither and yon: An old-fashioned way to say near and far.
horoscope: Predictions about a person's future based on the positions of the planets and stars at a given time (*horo-* means hour; a *scope* is a means of observation).
hors d'oeuvres: (pronounced "ôr-dûrv'-z ə") Appetizers or fancy bits of food served before a meal.
hunching: Bending over or squatting.
hunt him: Here it means take him hunting.
husky: Strong and rugged.
hype: Overrating something in order to sell it.
hypocrisy: Pretending to have certain beliefs or virtues (*hypo-* means under or incomplete).
hysterical: Showing uncontrollable emotion.
I'm no hand at writing: I'm not a very good writer.
illuminated: Lit up (*il-* means in; *-lumin-* means light).
illustrate: Explain something by using examples (*-lus-* refers to light).
immerse: Completely cover with or submerge in a liquid (*im-* means in; *-merse* refers to dipping).
immigrant: A person who comes into a country to live permanently (*im-* means in; *-migra-* refers to moving). This label is different from the refugee label, which means that the person does not have a country to go to for a period of time.
immune: Here it means not affected by or responsive to surroundings.
immunity: The state of not being affected by something.

imperative: Very necessary.
imperceptible: Not noticeable (*im-* means not; *-cep-* refers to seizing or grasping).
imperceptibly: Not noticeably (here *im-* means not; *-percept-* refers to noticeable). "They nod slightly" is a clue.
imperious: Urgent or commanding (*imperi-* refers to an empire).
impersonal: Not personal (*im-* here means not).
inaudible: Not able to be heard (*in-* here means not; *-aud-* refers to hearing).
inaudible: Incapable of being heard.
incentive: Something causing one to be active or to put forth effort.
inevitably: Without the possibility of being avoided.
infirmity: Illness or weakness (*in-* here means not; *-firm-* means firm or strong).
ingenuity: Cleverness.
inquiring: Asking (*-quir-* refers to asking).
inspiration: Something that encourages another to act (*in-* means into; *-spira-* refers to breathing).
instill: Firmly establish.
instinctively: With inborn knowledge (*in-* means within).
intercession: A plea (in this case to God) on behalf of others (*inter-* means between; *-ces-* refers to going).
interlock: Join closely together (*inter-* means between or among).
intermittency: The state of stopping and starting again (*inter-* means between; *-mit-* means to send).
intervened: Here it means came between two points of time (*inter-* means between; *-ven-* means to come).
intimacy: Here it means the state of physical or sexual closeness to another person.
intimate: Familiar or close.
intolerable: Unbearable (*in-* here means not; *-toler-* means to bear). Related to tolerate which means to bear or put up with.
invade: Enter by force (*in-* here means in; *-vad-* means to go).
invariably: Unchangingly (*in-* here means not; *variable* means changeable).
invigorated: Given strength or vigor.
itinerary: The route proposed for a journey.
jade: A gemstone that is usually green.
jams: Crowded masses.
keen: Here it means strong.
keening: Loud wailing.
kneaded: (pronounced "ne-d-id") Here it means squeezed or massaged. "...his legs against cramp" is a clue.
knobby: Having knobs or large bumps sticking out.
laboring: Working with great effort.
languid: Without energy; slow
lashed out: Attacked or threatened.
latter: The second of two items mentioned.
lead: The British word for leash (the leather strap or rope used to control a dog).
lean years: Years when there is not much money to provide the necessities of living.
leeway: Greater freedom.
let it go at that: Didn't continue with a discussion or thought.
litter: The baby animals produced during one birth.
lodge: Here it means a building in which American Indian religious ceremonies are often held.
ludicrous: Absurd or laughable.

luminous: Giving off light (*lumin-* means light).

lute: A musical instrument that is pear-shaped and has strings.

macadam: A highway made of layers of small stones and tar.

make it on his own: Live independently.

making double time: Getting paid double the regular pay.

making the ends meet: Managing to live with a limited amount of money.

malignant: Very harmful (*mal-* means bad or evil).

maligned: (pronounced "mə-lin'-d") Defamed or slandered.

manipulation: Here it means the act of using one's hands skillfully (*man-* means hand).

mantle: A cover.

mariachis: Mexican street musicians.

mediums: Here it means individuals who claim to have the power to communicate with the dead.

mellowed: Become full-flavored and rich tasting; not harsh or bitter.

memoirs: A collection of personal experiences written down so that they may not be forgotten (*mem-* refers to remembering).

menacing: Threatening.

menial: Typical of a servant.

merely: Only.

merge: Blend together, losing individual identity.

mesh: Here it means the bringing together of.

metallic: Like metal.

methodically: In a regular or systematic order (a *method* is a set of orderly procedures).

migration: Here it means a seasonal move to another region (*migrate* means to move).

mincingly: Here it means walking with short steps (*min-* refers to small).

minding of the store: Managing of the store.

moccasins: Leather slippers traditionally made and worn by American Indians.

mode: A way of doing something.

monotonous: Without variety (*mono-* means one).

move along something: Here it means to give something to someone else.

muffled: Deadened by a covering. ". . . covered his head with her shawl" is a clue.

multilingual: Able to speak several languages (*multi-* means several; *-ling-* refers to language).

multiplicity: The state of being varied and/or in large number.

murmur: The low sound of voices, slightly above a whisper.

muses: Here it means brings about a state of thought.

mutual: Felt or shared equally by two or more people.

mysteriously: In a way that is full of mystery.

mystify: Greatly puzzle (*mysti-* refers to secrecy).

nonnegotiable: Not capable of being changed as part of a compromise.

norm: The thing that is standard or the average.

nucleus: The center.

nurture: Here it means encourage or promote the development of (*nurt-* refers to feeding).

nurturing: Helping to develop

nutrient: That which helps something to grow and develop. It often refers to food.

oak tree: A tree bearing acorns (a type of nut).

obligations: Duties (*ob-* means to; *-liga-* means to bind).

obsessive: Having a fixed, unreasonable idea that often causes anxiety

occupant: One who lives in or occupies something.

old-timer: A person who has lived a long time.

onslaught: Attack (*slaught-* refers to striking or hitting).

oppressed: Weighed heavily upon or depressed (*op-* means against).

orgies: Parties at which people give in to their immediate desires, showing little self-control.

outset: Beginning.

outwitted: Outsmarted or defeated by superior cleverness (*wit* here means intelligence).

overwhelm: Overcome or overpower.

pact: An agreement.

padding: Walking with soft steps.

is a clue.

pang: A sudden, intense feeling or rush of emotion.

pasture: An open field upon which grow grasses and other plants eaten by grazing animals.

patronage: Support, encouragement, or protection (a patron is someone who gives patronage; *pat-* refers to father).

peered: Looked.

peppering: Sprinkling as though with pepper.

peremptorily: Here it means commandingly.

perennial: Appearing over and over again.

persisted: Stood firm (*per-* here means completely; *-sist-* refers to standing firm).

petulant: Showing a bad temper.

picked their way: Went slowly and carefully to avoid obstacles.

picked: Here it means opened with a pick (a sharp tool).

pilgrimage: A journey for an important, sometimes sacred, purpose (a pilgrim is a traveler).

pillars: Columns or vertical structures used for support.

pines: a type of evergreen tree.

pitched headlong: Fell swiftly, head first.

placidly: Calmly (*plac-* refers to pleasing).

plodded: Moved with heavy steps.

plucked out: Pulled out abruptly.

plunged: Moved suddenly and with much force.

poignant: (pronounced "p-oin-yent") Keenly or intensely felt.

poring through: Here it means reading carefully.

porpoise: A small whale with a rounded snout.

precepts: Principles

precisely: Exactly.

prep school: A school that prepares students for college.

pricked: Here it means made to stand up. It also means pierced or poked.

prided: Took pride in.

primary: Here it means most important (*prim-* means first).

procession: A group of people or things moving forward in a line (*pro-* means forward; *-ces-* refers to going).

profound: Deep.

pronounced: Here it means noticeable.

prophet: One who predicts the future (*pro-* means before).

propped up: Leaned against something for support.

protested: Strongly objected.

psychiatric: Related to the medical treatment of mental illness (*psychi-* refers to the spirit or soul).

pulsate: Move to a strong beat (*puls-* means to beat).

pulse: Heartbeat.

puma: A mountain lion.

punching a time clock: Placing a card in a machine that records the exact time. A time clock is used to record how many hours a person has worked.

pursue: Follow.

quadruple: Having four parts (*quad-* means four).

quaint: Old-fashioned in a pleasing way.

quartered: Divided something into four equal parts.

quiver: To shake rapidly or vibrate.

rabbi: An official religious leader of the Jewish faith.

rafters: Boards that support a roof.

rapt: Completely involved.

raw: Here it means inexperienced.

receded: Here it means seemed farther away.

recurring: Happening again and again (*re-* means back; *-curr-* means run).

red tape: Massive paperwork (forms to fill out, etc.).

reeling: Being thrown off balance.

refuge: Here it means an escape.

refugee camp: A place where people who do not have a country to go to can live temporarily and receive basic necessities for living.

regret: A feeling of grief and sorrow.

relinquishments: Things given up or left behind (*re-* here means behind; *-linquish-* refers to leaving).

remote: Far away (*re-* means back or away; *-mote* refers to moving).

rendered: Gave back; yielded.

renegade: A person who has rejected one group or tradition in favor of another.

resentment: A feeling of anger toward something or someone thought to be the cause of one's emotional or physical pain.

restraining: Holding back.

restraint: Something that limits or prevents movement (to *restrain* means to hold back).

retreating: Going back or withdrawing (*re-* here means back).

retreats: Backs away.

reveries: Daydreams.

reviews: Here it means reports in newspapers or magazines that tell the reporters' views of the strengths and weaknesses of a piece of work.

reviving: Bringing back to life (*re-* means again; *-viv-* refers to life).

revolves: Moves in a circle (*re-* here means back; *-volve-* refers to rolling).

rigid: Not bending or moving (*rigi-* refers to stiff).

rouse: Bring to attention or awaken.

ruffled: Disturbed.

running his heart out: Running as fast as possible, with all his energy.

ruptured: Broken open (*rupt-* means to break).

rustle: A whispering sound.

rustled: Whispering sounds caused by surfaces coming together.

rutted: Having deep tracks usually made by the wheels of vehicles.

sandpipers: Small wading birds with long legs.

savor: Here it means something that adds zest or excitement.

scampering: Running hurriedly or playfully.

scholar: A highly educated person (*schol-* means school).

scoops: Here it means rounded cavities or holes.

scorn: Anger and disgust.

scrabbled: Made quick, scraping movements.

scurried: Moved quickly, with light, short steps.

sea anemone: (pronounced "a-nem-a-ne-") A very brightly colored, flowerlike animal that sits at the bottom of the sea. It has thin arms or tentacles that sway invitingly around its large hidden mouth.

seances: Meetings at which people are said to receive messages from the dead through a medium.

seasoned: Here it means dried enough to be usable as firewood.

seclusion: The state of being apart from others or secluded.

seductive: Powerfully tempting (*se-* means apart or away from; *-duc-* means to lead).

segregated: Separated (*se-* means apart; *-greg-* refers to a herd or flock).

sensation: Here it means bodily feeling.

sentence of death: A pronouncement that one must die for something one has done or failed to do.

serenade: Perform music for someone, usually one's lover.

serene: Calm.

shackles: Metal rings placed around the wrists or ankles to hinder movement.

shawls: Loose coverings women sometimes wear over their heads and shoulders to provide warmth.

sheaths: Coverings.

shed: Here it means gotten rid of or caused to fall off.

sheer: Here it means not mixed with anything; pure.

shred: Here it means a thin strip.

shrugged: Here it means raised the shoulders to show uncertainty.

shudder: A trembling as if from great fear.

shuttle: Travel back and forth.

sideshow: A show performed in addition to the main show.

sidled: Moved sideways.

signaled: Communicated or indicated without words.

signing: Here it means using signs formed by fingers and hands to communicate ideas. Such sign language is used by the deaf and those who communicate with the deaf.

silhouetted: (pronounced "sil-oo-et-id") Appearing to be outlined and filled in with black.

simile: A comparison using the word *like* or *as*.

singed: Burned on the edges.

skim: To move swiftly over a surface, barely touching it.

slicked: Smoothed down, usually with an oily substance.

slipcovers: Protective covers that are put over furniture.

slippered progress: Wearing slippers and progressing or moving forward.

slitted: Made of narrow strips of material with spaces between them.

sluggards: Slow-moving persons.

smock: A loose, lightweight coatlike covering worn to protect one's clothes while working.

snaillike: Like a snail: a small, soft, slow-moving creature whose shell comes to a point. It lives on land or in water.

snug: Cozy and secure.

solemn: Very serious.

solemnly: Deeply serious.

solidity: The state of being solid.

solitude: Being by oneself (*soli-* refers to being alone).

spasmodically: In uncontrollable bursts or spasms, which are sudden muscle contractions.

spiral: A shape that circles upward around a central point (a *spire* is a point or the highest part).

spiritualists: Here it means people who claim that the dead can communicate with the living.

sprawled: Spread out in a disordered way.

spruce: An evergreen tree having needles and cones.

squarely: Here it means directly.

squatted: Sat on one's heels.

squeamish: Easily sickened.

staggered: Moved unsteadily from side to side.

stalked: Here it means walked or moved angrily.

stalwart: Here it means not giving up physically or mentally.

standard of living: The economic level at which one lives.

steer: A type of ox.

still life: An art style in which all subjects are lifeless.

stoop: Here it means a small porch or platform.

strained: Used great effort to hear.

straitjackets: Jackets that bind one's arms tightly to the sides of the body in order to prevent their movement (*strait-* refers to pulling tightly together).

strode: Moved with long, confident steps (the past tense of stride).

strove: Worked hard toward some goal (the past tense of *strive*).

submersion: The state of being completely covered by or under the surface of something (*sub-* means under).

sufficient: Enough.

suicide: The act of killing oneself (*sui-* refers to self; *-cide* means killing).

sulfur: A yellow chemical used to make matches.

summit: Highest point.

surge: Here it means a sudden rush from inside (*sur-* means up from below).

surveyed: Looked over carefully.

sushi-ized: An invented word similar to the word "modernized" (*sushi* is raw fish; *-ized* here means to be accepted as a practice).

suspect: (pronounced here "sá-spekt"). Here it means doubted.

swaying: Moving back and forth in a swinging motion.

tag along: Go along with or follow.

taken for granted: Assumed to always be available.

teens: Ages thirteen through nineteen.

terrace: A platform forming a type of porch or patio.

the other side of the coin: The opposite of something.

the old country: The country from which one's ancestors came.

thrashed: Moved about wildly.

threshing: Thrashing or moving wildly about.

throttle: Here it means choke.

tides: The rising and falling of the surface levels of a body of water due to the forces of gravity.

toil-slave: Work-slave.

token: A small sample standing for the whole thing.

tonic: Something that gives vitality.

tottered: Lost balance.

treacherous: Very dangerous; misleading (*treach-* refers to trick).

trepidation: A state of fearfulness.

tribute: A show of respect and admiration (*trib-*

trotted: Moved at a fast pace between walking and running.

trousers: The British word for pants.

trudged: Walked as though one's feet were very heavy.

trunks: Men's shorts used for swimming.

tuition: The money that a person pays to go to a public college or university or to a private school.

twilight: The soft, dim light that fills the sky after sunset (*twi-* here means half).

twittered: Chirped lightly.

ulcerous: Like an open sore.

unveiled: Here it means demonstrated openly to be viewed by all.

upside/downside: Positive side/negative side.

upstate: The northern part of the state.

utterly: Completely.

vanity: The state of being vain or paying too much attention to appearance.

vantage point: A position giving advantage.

vaseline: An oily, greasy substance.

vaudeville: A type of show consisting of a series of short acts performed for the entertainment of others.

vexatious: (pronounced "vek-sa'-shəs") Annoying or disturbing.

vices: Here it means bad habits.

Virgo: One of the many signs of the zodiac. The zodiac is a diagram showing the imaginary paths of the planets. People born between August 23 and September 22 are said to be Virgos.

vitality: Liveliness or energy (*vita-* means life).

voluble: Fluent.

weary: Very tired.

welter: Confusion.

whence: An old-fashioned way to say "from where."

whimper: Cry or sob softly.

whine: Give out a high-pitched cry.

whiplash: A whip used to hit the dogs pulling a sled to make them run faster.

wholesome: Healthy.

willed: Here it means wanted.

winch: A machine used to move heavy objects or cargo.

wires: Here it refers to the connections between the brain and the fingers.

wisps: Small fragments.

wistfulness: The state of being wishful.

with all his might: With all his strength.

wrenched: Suddenly twisted.

wrestling: Struggling or fighting in close body contact in an effort to bring another to the floor.

yearnings: Desires.

yield: Give in or surrender.

CREDITS

Grateful acknowledgment is given to the following publishing companies and individuals for permission to reprint or adapt materials for which they own copyrights:

To a Distant Shore Autobiographical sketches adapted from *Home of the Brave* by Mary Motley Kalergis. Foreword by Cornell Capa. Copyright ©1989 by Mary Motley Kalergis, Foreword copyright ©1989 by Cornell Capa. Used by permission of the publisher, Dutton, an imprint of New American Library, a division of Penguin Books USA Inc.

The Journey Back Lyrics from the song *First Christmas*, by Stan Rogers. From *Between the Breaks . . . Live!* courtesy of Fogarty's Cove Music, Inc.; Excerpt from "Blue Winds Dancing" by Thomas Whitecloud from *Scribner's Magazine*, Volume CIII, Number 2, February 1938. Copyright ©1938 Charles Scribner's Sons; Copyright renewed. Adapted with permission of Charles Scribner's Sons, an imprint of Macmillan Publishing Company.

Letting Go "The Red Dog" by Howard Earl Maier appeared in *Colliers*, Vol. 124, September 10, 1949, and in *Scholastic*, Vol. 55, Oct. 12, 1949. "Leaving Home" by Wendy Abbott Hansen. Used by permission of the author.

All That Glitters "Carmel Point" by Margaret Phyllis MacSweeney. Copyright ©1930 Scholastic Magazine, Inc. in *Reflections on a Gift of Watermelon Pickle . . .* by Stephen Dunning, Edward Lueders, Hugh Smith, ©1966, Scott, Foresman & Co. Excerpt from *The Pearl* by John Steinbeck. Copyright © renewed 1973 by Elaine Steinbeck, Thom Steinbeck and John Steinbeck IV. Used by permission of Viking Penguin, a division of Penguin Books USA Inc. Song "Richard Cory" copyright © 1966 by Paul Simon. Used by permission of the publisher.

The Power of Illusion Houdini's story adapted from "Man of Mystery and Magic" by Lester David. Originally published *in Boy's Life* 1968. Used by permission of Lester David. "The Sword-Swallower" poem and drawing by Shel Silverstein from *A Light in the Attic*, copyright © 1981 by Evil Eye Music, Inc. Used by permission of Edite Kroll Literary Agency.

Between Two Cultures Poem "Second Nature" by Diana Chang, published in *The New York Quarterly*, Spring 1972, by the National Poetry Foundation, Orono, Maine 04469; Adaptation of "Cecilia Rosas" by Amado Muro first appeared in *New Mexico Quarterly*, Vol. XXXIV, No. 4, Winter 1964.

The Search for Love "The Rose" by Amanda McBroom copyright © 1977 Warner-Tamerlane Publishing Corp. & Third Story Music Inc. All rights reserved. Used by permission; From "Romantic Deceptions and Reality" adapted from *False Love and Other Romantic Illusions* by Dr. Stan J. Katz and Aimee E. Liu. Copyright by Dr. Stan Katz and Aimee E. Liu. Reprinted by permission of Ticknor & Fields, a Houghton Mifflin Co. imprint. All rights reserved; Excerpt from "The Prophet" by Kahlil Gibran. Copyright © 1923 by Kahlil Gibran and renewed 1951 by administrators C.T.A. of Kahlil Gibran Estate and Mary G. Gibran. Reprinted by permission of Alfred A. Knopf, Inc.

Survival Excerpt from "To Build a Fire" by Jack London, from *Lost Faces*. Published by Macmillan; Biographical sketch adapted from "Steven K. Chough" by Gareth Heibert in *Tributes to Courage*. Copyright © 1980 by Courage Center, Golden Valley, Minnesota.

Simple Pleasures From *The Essential Calvin & Hobbes* by Bill Watterson. Copyright © 1988 Universal Press Syndicate; Excerpts from "Gift From the Sea" by Anne Morrow Lindbergh. Copyright 1955 by Anne Morrow Lindbergh. Reprinted by permission of Pantheon Books, a division of Random House, Inc; "I Have Found Such Joy" by Grace Noll Crowell, in *Best Loved Poems to Read Again and Again*, compiled by Mary Stanford Laurence. Copyright © 1979 by Hart Associates. Published in 1988 by Galahad Books, New York.

Images of Growing Old "The First Snow of the Year" by Mark van Doren from *Mark van Doren: 100 Poems*. Copyright © 1967 by Mark van Doren. Reprinted by permission of Hill and Wang, a division of Farrar, Straus and Giroux, Inc; "Always Ahead," an essay by Elizabeth Yates, is adapted from *The Courage to Grow Old*, edited by Phillip L. Berman. Copyright © 1989 by The Center For Study of Contemporary Belief, Denver, CO 80203. Reprinted by permission of Ballantine Books, a division of Random

(continued)

House, Inc.; "Desiderata," copyright © 1927 by Max Ehrmann. Copyright renewed 1954 by Bertha K. Ehrmann. Reprinted by permission of Robert L. Bell, Melrose, MA 02176.

Grateful acknowledgment is given to the following for providing artwork or photographs:

pages 4,7,9,10 by Mary Motley Kalergis in *Home of the Brave;*

page 18 Old Sturbridge Village photo by Robert S. Arnold;

page 29 Irish Setter Ch. Tague's Son of Erin, owner/breeder Catherine J.T. Hill;

page 44 used by permission of Greenpeace Communications Ltd., London;

pages 61, 65 from *Houdini: A Pictorial Life* by Milbourne Christopher, Thomas Y. Crowell Company. Copyright © 1976 by Milbourne Christopher;

page 71 Drawing by Shel Silverstein, copyright 1981, Evil Eye Music, Inc., and the Edite Kroll Literary Agency;

page 74 Anita Wong. Used by permission of Anita Wong.

page 89 David Brownell, © 1986 State of New Hampshire;

page 99 *Single Slices* cartoons by Peter Kohlsaat, copyright © Los Angeles Times Syndicate. Reprinted with permission. LUANN cartoon by Greg Evans, reprinted with special permission of North American Syndicate;

page 102 photo by W. Jack Schick, from *Alaska & the Yukon,* Facts on File Publications;

page 116 copyright © 1980, Courage Center;

page 121 photo by Seastock Sammon, Croton-on-Hudson, NY;

page 121 CALVIN AND HOBBES copyright © 1986 Watterson. Dist. by Universal Press Syndicate. Reprinted with permission. All rights reserved.